Secrets of

THE BUSINESS

WEALTH

ACCELERATORS

33 MILLIONAIRES
MENTORS & MARKETERS
REVEAL THEIR STRATEGIES
FOR SUCCESS
IN THE NEW ECONOMY

From the Network of

PAUL AVINS

Founder of The Business Wealth Club

Published by Sunmakers, a division of Eldamar Ltd
in association with PA Enterprises
157 Oxford Road, Cowley, Oxford, OX4 2ES, UK
Tel +44(0)1865 779944

www.sunmakers.co.uk

Version 2.0

ISBN: 978-0-9559610-2-1

www.thebusinesswealthclub.com

DEDICATION

I want to dedicate this book to the woman in my life without whom I would never have had the courage and self belief to follow my dream and enter this amazing industry!

My wonderful wife - Sue Avins

She keeps my feet on the ground while encouraging me to shoot for the stars - a rare and priceless gift and one I am blessed to have in my life.

She is also a Kick Ass Project Manager without her this book would never have been pulled together in record time :-)

Thanks Babe, love you.

— *Paul Avins*

ACKNOWLEDGEMENTS

I would like to say a HUGE thank you to the people who have worked so hard to make this book a reality.

Ayd Instone for doing an AMAZING job on the cover design and the layout to really bring my vision to life. Angela and Lesley in my office for all their support and endless proof reading. To the members of my Oxford Wealth Club who have supported me and made our Open Day events so dynamic, leading to me becoming friends with many of the chapter authors.

Sue, for her skill and persistence project managing this in record time. Keeping me in line and ensuring that everybody delivered their content in time (not an easy task!). Finally to our Club Mentors, Dave, Steve C, Doug, Marcellus, Helena, Alan and Steve P for being part of our team and helping me spread my Business Support Systems to more people than I could ever reach on my own.

I would also like to thank each and every author you are about to meet and the event promoters who asked me to speak at the events that lead to many of these relationships coming into my life.

Pulling together a project like this is a true TEAM effort and I am blessed that so many amazing people brought their own personal magic to this book – I am so excited to share it with you.

Thank You all from the bottom of my heart.

— *Paul Avins*

CONTENTS
BY CONTRIBUTOR

LEIGH **ASHTON** 54
PAUL **AVINS** 16
BILL **BELEW** 94
STEVE **BROOKS** 62
NICK **CARLILE** 240
MARIE-CLAIRE **CARLYLE** 200
KIM **CASTLE & W. VITO MOTONE** 24
MICHELLE **CLARKE** 32
RON **DAVIES** 102
MARCUS **DE MARIA** 248
BERNIE **DE SOUZA** 70
GARY **FOX** 110
ALAN **FRENCH** 38
DAVE **GRIFFIN** 118
NICK **GRIFFITH** 76
ANDREW **GRIFFITHS** 46
DOUG **HECKER** 82
DAVE **HOLLAND** 206
GAVIN **HOLMES** 256
HELENA **HOLRICK** 152
AYD **INSTONE** 162
SOHAIL **KHAN** 214
JEFF **LERMER** 220
MARCELLUS **LINDSAY** 228
JOANNA **MARTIN** 170
DANIEL **PRIESTLEY** 178
ANDREW **ROBERTS** 126
PETER **THOMSON** 184
SIMON **WALLACE-JONES** 134
DANIEL **WAGNER** 190
SIMON **K WILLIAMS** 144
SIMON **ZUTSHI** 264

CONTENTS
BY TOPIC

BUSINESS GROWTH

14

16 THE IMPORTANCE OF A BALANCED BUSINESS EDUCATION

24 BRAND CREATION FOR THE NEW ECONOMY

32 TEAM SPORTS

38 AN EXPEDITION INTO LEADERSHIP

46 THE AGE OF THE ENTREPRENEUR

LEVERAGED INVESTMENTS

238

240 MAXIMISING YOUR RETURNS FROM PROPERTY

248 STOCK MARKET INVESTING

256 HOW TO LOSE MONEY AS A TRADER & INVESTOR

264 PROPERTY INVESTING

270 THE BUSINESS WEALTH CLUB

MONEY & MARGINS

198

200 HOW TO BECOME A MONEY MAGNET

206 CONTRADICTION BY NUMBERS

214 HOW TO CONNECT WITH MILLIONAIRES AND BILLIONAIRES

220 KEEPING HOLD OF THE MONEY YOU MAKE

228 IMPLEMENTATION OF IDEAS DRIVES YOUR INCOME!

SALES & MARKETING
52

THE NEW INGREDIENTS OF SALES SUCCESS 54

THE HIDDEN SOURCE OF NEW CUSTOMERS 62

MORE CLIENTS WITHOUT EVEN SELLING 70

SUCCESSFUL JOINT VENTURES 76

THE 7 SECRETS TO ENTREPRENEURIAL ENLIGHTENMENT 82

ONLINE MARKETING
92

GET TRAFFIC TO YOUR WEB SITE 94

FACEBOOK FOR OFFLINE BUSINESS 102

WHY BRANDS USE FACEBOOK 110

SUPERCHARGE YOUR SOCIAL MEDIA 118

CREATE SALES FROM WEBINARS 126

SOCIAL MEDIA BUTTONS 134

HOW TO PROFIT FROM MOBILE APPS 144

EXPERT POSITIONING
150

HOW TO BE A WORKSHOP WIZARD 152

EXPERTISE BRANDING 162

HOW TO USE SPEAKING TO GROW YOUR BUSINESS 170

BECOME A KEY PERSON OF INFLUENCE 178

CREATE AND MARKET INFORMATION PRODUCTS 184

PACKAGING SECRETS FOR INFORMATION PRODUCTS 190

FORW

BY PAUL AVINS

Firstly - Forward is NOT a typo! With all of the Energy and Momentum contained within this book.... this is the only way I could kick off your journey!

In the last few years we have lived through the biggest Credit bubble and now the biggest debt crisis for almost 70 years, meaning that the good old days of predictable year-on-year growth are gone for good.

So, what is the fall-out from this economic shift? Investors are leaving the stock market at record levels, residential and commercial property around the world has lost 30, 40 and in some cases over 50% of its value, and may drop even further. Governments are fighting off financial disaster on a weekly basis, and even the USA has had its 3 star credit rating downgraded!

The main engine for growth in the economy for the last 30 years, the baby boomers, are reaching a time in their lives where they are shifting their focus from spending to saving causing *big* changes in consumer habits.

YET - amongst all this negative news, financial fear and the debt disasters, there are people just like you, generating enormous wealth in all its different forms.

I know of many Businesses growing by 50, 60 even 100+ % in markets that are apparently "depressed"! Owners selling their companies for millions. Investors making *huge* returns in the markets, trading shares and currencies. Internet based marketers continue to generate millions in sales and profits with no more than a laptop and a mobile phone.

Joint venture industries are being born almost daily and generating millions. Property investors are building asset wealth and positive cash flow at record speed in specific markets and locations, and rents are outstripping inflation.

New economic powers are rising up and growing at staggering levels such as Brazil, Russia, India, and China, (known as BRIC countries) as well as markets like South Africa and Turkey...

Today where you choose to FOCUS will determine your financial future but you'll need to evaluate your strategies and pick a mix that works for you.

By picking up or downloading this book I know you are the type of person who, like the authors in this book, can see opportunities everywhere.

This book is giving you direct access to my personal, and up until now very private wealth network. These experts have all helped me and my private coaching clients to accelerate our wealth of *ideas, skills, relationships, team members, suppliers, knowledge, working capital, cash flow, leads, sales, customers, profits, joint venture partners*, and critically *wealth network* and *personal wealth* in recent years.

Who are they? Well over the last 7 years I have had the huge privilege of getting to know and work with the *millionaires, mentors* and *marketers* you're about to meet and learn from in this amazing book.

Sometimes sharing a stage with them at big multi-speaker seminars around the world or as my guest at our Business Wealth Club Open Days. Sometimes as their business coach, getting to help them take their businesses to the next level. Sometimes as their student to expand my knowledge in a specific area. But always as their friend and kindred spirit on a similar journey to learn the HOW of *wealth acceleration*. After all, the *why* is staring us all in the wallet!

The biggest learning I've had many times over my 7 year career as a business coach is that *success leaves clues!* So I spent a long time hand-picking and selecting experts to invite into this book. I needed people who were not only considered at the top of their game (which they are), but also who I knew aligned with my values; who shared my desire to bring about positive change in a world where so many people are scared for their financial future, their jobs and their security in retirement.

Let's be honest, the media gets high on the distribution of bad news, horror and fear and there is little time given to the opposing view of opportunity, contribution and hope.

So my response to the negative media led culture of fear is this book!

To empower people just like you with real world "how to" knowledge so you can take action and create the lifestyle, business or financial returns of your dreams.

HOW TO USE THIS BOOK

This book has been divided into specific themed sections so that you can either read all the way through and decide which strategy appeals to your personality type and natural talents. Or if you know what your passion is, you can just head to that section first and devour the information there.

I would STRONGLY suggest that whatever your preferred wealth creation focus is, you also read the section on business. In my experience coaching and mentoring millionaires over the years, they all, without exception, view business as their central wealth acceleration strategy. Only once they built strong predictable cash flow did they start redeploying profits into other strategies like property, stocks and shares or other business ventures... just as many of the people on the Times Rich List have done over the years.

> I was once asked at a seminar by a member of the audience what they should do with the £60k they had to invest? My answer was invest in enough self education so that they didn't need to ask me such a crazy question!

The only person who should decide what strategies you use and implement is YOU. I say this because you have the most to lose if they don't work out and the most to gain if they do. You must take Personal Responsibility for this part of your life, it's too important to *outsource* or delegate.

To *accelerate your levels of learning*, after all this book is all about speeding up your results and time is ticking away for all of us, which is why I suggest the following:

SET YOUR LEARNING GOALS NOW – BY ANSWERING THESE QUESTIONS:

- Why are you reading this book?

- What results are you looking to achieve to create wealth in your life in the next 5 years?

- What specific information do you want to learn from this book?

- Who could you teach this information to after you have read it? (It's proven we learn best when we have to organise our thinking to teach somebody)

- How will you know when you've applied the information you've learned?

- How will you feel when you have secured your financial future?

I'l be pointing out my key learnings – you need to do the same!

READ WITH A HIGHLIGHTER IN YOUR HAND AND PULL OUT THE KEY POINTS

You'll notice that I've put Post-It notes next to some of what I think are a few of the key messages to help give you some coaching and get you started. The chapters are packed with gold nuggets waiting to be discovered by you. Highlight the ones that jump out at you to lock in the learning plus you can find them again quickly.

> **Have a note book, iPad or laptop handy to write notes on key ideas and plan the ACTIONS you'll take.**

Whole brain learning is a powerful tool for accumulating a lot of information quickly. We use it in all our training sessions at The Business Wealth Club, taking lots of notes is one of these strategies.

USE THE 72 HOUR RULE

If it's a great idea start using it within 72 hours or forget it and move on. Enough said!

PLAN TO RE-READ THIS BOOK A NUMBER OF TIMES

Don't imagine for one second that you'll learn everything on the first pass. We have a saying that repetition is the mother of learning, and at the Business Wealth Club meetings, we often find it's when members hear something for the second or third time they finally "get it". After all you'll be in a different place every time you revisit the chapters and different ideas will resonate.

HAVE AN OPEN MIND

Try and put aside any pre-conceived ideas you have about wealth creation. One of the most exciting things about the chapters in this book is that some of the experts actually contradict each other. What this means to me is that there is more than one road to your "success" destination – take the directions that feel right to you, and don't be afraid to re-calculate your route mid–journey.

At the end of the book you'll find a guide to creating your *Wealth Acceleration Action Plan*™ to keep you fuelled up, focused and generating results faster than you ever thought possible.

> **As we like to say to our Business Wealth Club members at the end of every meeting - You get paid on what you get DONE!**

Enjoy the ride and I look forward to reading or hearing about your results. Put your foot down and lets get started...

WE ARE IN A NEW AGE:
ENTREPRENEURSHIP FUELLED
BY TECHNOLOGY AND A DESIRE
FOR PERSONAL FREEDOM. NOW
MORE THAN EVER, RUNNING
YOUR OWN BUSINESS CAN BE AT
THE HEART OF YOUR WEALTH
CREATION STRATEGY, LET US
TEACH YOU HOW...

BUSI
GRO

NESS
VTH

PAUL
AVINS

He is to business what a Turbocharger is to a car – He boosts bottom line results – Fast!

Paul is an award winning Business Growth Coach, Author of Business SOS, International Speaker, creator of the Turbo Growth System™ and Founder of the world's first blended Learning & Networking Franchise, The Business Wealth Club.

His personal track record includes starting, building and selling a number of his own businesses, losing it all in the Dot.com crash and having to start over again!

Paul loves to take his own brand of high energy coaching, personal development and powerful, simple to implement tools out to business owners and entrepreneurs' wanting faster results, and has shared the stage with experts including James Caan, Rachel Elnaugh, David Gold, Mike Southon, Michael Gerber as well as many of the authors in this book!

Most recently he is proud of the work he has done with some exciting clients including VW, Salon Success, Paul Mitchell and Porsche as well as the results he has achieved working in over 79 different industries generating over £109 million in additional sales and profits for his private coaching clients.

When he's not working Paul loves spending time with his wife Sue and their son Jonathan James (JJ) usually getting beaten at Star Wars Lego on the Wii!

THE IMPORTANCE OF A BALANCED BUSINESS EDUCATION

As you can imagine, I have sat at the back of a lot of Seminar, Workshop and Wealth Club rooms over the years, but am still always thrilled to go – I never get tired of seeing the difference that Paul can facilitate for people, it's an honour to be a spectator.

To me, Paul's unique skill is that in any given situation, (whether he's talking to one Mentoring Client – or stood on stage in front of 2000 people), he has the uncanny ability to read the situation and "pluck" different pieces of content and knowledge from seemingly unconnected courses he has been on, books that he's read, or maybe even situations other clients have been in – and weave them together in a new way that is just what the ears in front of him need to hear at that time.

So, open your ears to learning and let Paul share his key ideas with you...

— Sue Avins

BUSINESS GROWTH

17

> **One of the big mistakes I've seen most business owners make over the years is to think that their current level of education will see them through the dynamic changing world of business that we live in.**

This is usually because they think that running a business is about the knowledge they have for being able to do the "job" of that business. Not true!

When they start to appreciate the real level of knowledge they are going to need, some entrepreneurs head for the hills, while others pay the ultimate price for their lack of a broad business education and go bust. A few smart Business Owners seek out Coaching, Mentoring and Support to bridge the gap.

Shockingly, 80% of Start Up's don't make it to the 5 year point! Now imagine if somebody told you those were the odds before you got on a plane – would you fly?

When I first got involved in personal development and realised that if I wanted to earn more I needed to Learn more – the impact was almost immediate and I saw my sales increase.

Some professions like accountants and lawyers force their members to complete a minimum number of Continuing Personal Development (CPD) hours to remain current and up to speed on changes to the Law etc. Just think about the financial success these professions enjoy. It's no accident. The crazy thing is that as Business Owners nobody forces us to keep learning new skills.

When I started The Business Wealth Club over 7 years ago, I wanted to create an education based Networking Club that was structured to give our members a *Balanced Business Education ™*.

What do I mean by this?

I mean being able to understand ALL the critical functions within your business, not just Sales & Marketing for example.

Lets take a look at the 8 Strategic and Tactical areas we build our meetings and members education around.

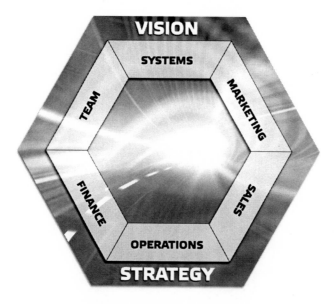

As we go through these together I suggest, as your coach, that you mark how good your skill and knowledge level is for each area with 1 being very poor, 10 being excellent.

This way you'll be benchmarking your current skill levels and will get a perspective on where you need to invest time and learning to grow your business.

OK lets start with:

VISION

The big picture first. Where do you want your business to be in the next 3/5 years? What Sales and Profits will you be making? What countries will you be operating in? What markets will you be serving? How many people will be working for you? Do you want to sell the business for asset wealth or build it for a lucrative lifestyle?

These questions are critical, as without a destination we just end up going round in circles. Think about it, would you get into a car to go on holiday with no idea of the destination? What chance have you got of getting there at all?

BUSINESS GROWTH

19

STRATEGY

Now we know your destination, we can start to evaluate and plan HOW we pull it off. It amazes me how many of our members over the years have joined with a great vision – but no documented plan to navigate by. Do you have one right now that you look at on your wall every day?

I've always believed that if you can't get your plan onto one page - it's not clear enough. This is why 4 times a year we hold 90 Day Roadmap to Results™ sessions with our members. It gets them focused on what they need to stop doing in the business that's not working? Complete a SWOT analysis (Strengths, Weaknesses, Opportunities and Threats) and review their Business Engine's™ performance, before planning their action steps for success.

Attend one and see how Great they are!

MARKETING

OK, this is one of my personal favourites to study, and as a business owner your ability to generate leads into your business is one of the greatest skills you'll need to master. It's so important that I've dedicated a whole chapter in this book to it, laying down the most cutting edge strategies that are currently getting great results. Branding is now more important than ever, which is why several of the experts also have chapters on this. (Funny thing is they all reference Apple as a company that "get it".)

During the year we delve deeper into this area with workshops, online video trainings and check lists etc. When we launch a new club in a town we run our *7 Sins of Marketing* workshop as a free taster session – it's definitely my favourite and is always a hit with the prospective Members in the room.

People always get revved up when they realise just how much there is to learn on this subject that can be applied to their business.

SALES

If you're not great at Sales, you are going to have a tough time getting new customers! This area has changed so much in the last 7 years with new tools like Social Media for prospecting; new ways of getting client referrals and testimonials to help your conversion rates skyrocket - using videos from happy clients on your website for example ☺

Many of the business owners we train in our *Speed Selling System*™ find that just investing some time detailing and documenting their features, advantages and benefits (FAB's) gives them the clarity to articulate the value they provide in a way potential customers understand so they no longer need to be "sold" – customers want to buy.

This workshop Rocks!

OPERATIONS

Having made the sale, the work really starts. What levels of customer service show up for all customers? What is your new client welcome pack like? Does every client, no matter how big or small receive the amazing experience they expect?

Now the game changes from making money when you make the sale, to keeping as much margin as possible during the delivery process. We use a great tool called the Profit Pipeline™ to help members see just where they are leaking money through poor service levels and inefficient distribution structures. Powerful stuff!

FINANCE

As I like to say "a sale is never a sale until the cash is in the bank". More businesses go bust because of the poor financial management, knowledge and skills of the owner than anything else.

Cash flow is like the oil in your car engine – no oil and it blows up fast. We recently ran a finance workshop, just to help all our members understand some of the terms and tools they need if they want to grow their wealth through building a business.

These tools include:

- Profit Budget

- Monthly Profit and Loss Statement

- Cash Flow Forecast

- Balance Sheet Statement

- Debtors & Creditors List

If you want some quick cash flow tips then check out my first book: *Business SOS – 173 Proven, Fast-Acting Strategies to take Your Business from Surviving to Thriving* , there is a whole chapter of tips on this subject in there!

TEAM

A huge myth that keeps many business owners stuck, as it did me for a while, is that I needed to become a Self Made Millionaire! So that meant doing everything myself!

No! No! No!

Every successful Millionaire I have coached and worked with over the years, and there have been quite a lot, will always say that they could not have done it without their team.

Or as I like to say "Teamwork makes your Dream Work!"

With the advent of websites like E-lance.com and Odesk.com you can "employ" contractors and freelance workers from all over the world on a project-by-project basis. This is a great way to keep your fixed costs down whilst giving you the ability to respond quickly in time of high customer demand.

One of the most frequent questions I get asked is "When should I recruit somebody into the admin role to get me out of this box?" A great question and my response often surprises people…

"When you can half afford somebody's salary for 90 days!"

90 days allows time to give them a test drive – and enables you to measure just how much extra you can get done to grow the business without the admin getting in the way.

SYSTEMS

For a business to be truly scalable (and therefore saleable), at some time you have to build and run it by the systems. After all think how crazy walking into a McDonalds would be if every teenager in there was left to do their own thing!

In fact don't think about it, its just too scary to imagine the mess!

Why are systems so powerful? Because they:

Save
You
Stress
Time
Energy &
Money

So, the more Systems you put in place to automate your Marketing, Sales, Operations, Finance, People Development and Training, the more Wealth, you receive in your life.

I look forward to meeting you soon at a Business Wealth Club meeting near you or at one of our events.

NEXT STEPS

To download your FREE business building pack worth £397 go to:

www.TheBusinessWealthClub.com

or connect with me online at:

www.Paul-Avins.com

www.twitter.com/turbobizcoach

www.facebook.com/paulavins

www.linkedin.com/In/paulavins

www.Oxford-BusinessWealthClub.co.uk

BUSINESS GROWTH

KIM CASTLE & W. VITO MOTONE

Kim Castle, international speaker, columnist, TV host and Brand Visioneer. She is co-creator (in partnership with Vito) of Intention Products LLC and BrandU®, a process-based, results-driven business helping entrepreneurs grow business effectively from idea to brand to market and Big Business Success No Matter Your Size, and the BrandU® Bible Workbook, It's A BrandU® Day, and Every Day Counts. Her passion lies in empowering entrepreneurs to realize their big business potential with the power of extreme clarity and Kim has helped thousands of small business owners around

the world translate their business ideas into marketable money-making brands with BrandU's three-stage Business Profit System.

W. Vito Montone, is a conscious business expert and leader in the pursuit of the whole wealth movement. He is also an award winning creative writer/producer with more than 25 years experience creating, producing and delivering entertainment and educational content for the stage, television, live events and interactive media and the Internet.

They are co-creators of Intention Products LLC, Castle Montone, Ltd. Why Communications and Interprise™ Business Academy. Intention Products is also offering free Conscious Business Development Kits featuring digital curriculum materials developed by BrandU®. Learn more at www.BrandU.com andhttp://blog.brandu.com/.

BRAND CREATION FOR THE NEW ECONOMY

I first saw Kim speak at *Mega Book Marketing University* in the US with the Author of *Chicken Soup for the Soul*, Mark Victor Hansen. I was blown away with her passion for helping business owners take their marketing results to a new level through the power of branding.

When I needed to create a new brand for me personally - Kim and Vito were the first people I called. I spent 3 months going through their Unique Branding process, a system I still reference today for projects, and "Paul Avins - Turbo Business Coach" was born! This brand alone helped me secure a number of 6 figure coaching contracts with some of the biggest names in the motor industry including VW, Porsche and Audi and their skills and approach can do the same for you!

— *Paul Avins*

The 21st century is an exciting time to be in business. Never before has the playing field been so level; via the Internet, both start-ups and global corporations can now cost-effectively reach a global audience — if they know the rules for this new economy.

> **With these opportunities, however, come new challenges, the largest being: How does any business stand out when there are millions of websites competing for attention over dozens of new distribution channels? Long-established marketing strategies are failing, and many businesses don't understand why.**

To succeed in the New Economy, every company, no matter how small, must create a viable brand — one that people connect to, one that will bring them back again and again to buy what the company is selling. This is true today more than at any other time in history.

Why? Because a new economy has evolved, driven in equal measure by the rise of social media, by an intense and prolonged global economic downturn, and by the seismic shift in expectations among consumers. Massive lay-offs have created thousands of new entrepreneurs competing to attract consumers who no longer buy anything that looks interesting, but only what they perceive to be valuable.

This is a key message!

For these newcomers, and for established businesses struggling to adjust, the New Economy demands a new way of approaching the concept of "brand," a sadly misunderstood concept.

Branding is the act of taking your message out to the consumer...on a frisbee, a pen, or on the side of a bus. It's the act of getting your brand seen.

Developing a brand means building something people will connect to for a lifetime. It is intrinsic to the core of your business and will directly determine your ability to reliably grow your business in the coming years by being so clear that you can cut straight through the mass of marketing noise.

Take Note!

No company is too small to develop their brand; in fact, success demands it from Day 1. You can begin today by following these five brand rules for the new economy:

BRAND RULE 1:
LEAD

Many marketers have said, "Find out what the market needs and then sell it." That approach may have worked in the dawn of Internet marketing, but it's not sustainable. News, information, and trends simply move too fast to stay ahead of such flux. Apple CEO Steve Jobs summed it up perfectly, "You can't just ask customers what they want and then try to give that to them. By the time you get it built, they'll want something new."

In order to command customer attention and loyalty, the new economy demands that you, the entrepreneur, get out in front with products and services that are innovative and become a vital part of consumers' lives. That comes from developing the *right* business.

The right business for you is one that connects to your core, that you love being a part of, and that solves a problem you are uniquely suited to solve. We all are uniquely suited to solve at least one problem and are on the path to solving it.

> Entrepreneurs who uncover their path turn into passionate communicators and are unstoppable in attracting the people who are best suited for their products and services.

BUSINESS GROWTH

> That inner passion is what sets your brand apart from everyone else and what frees you from trying to imitate your competitors. This has been proved by many successful companies...Whole Foods, Container Store, and, of course, Apple.

BRAND RULE 2: ONE-TO-MANY

In order to truly thrive in the new economy, you must understand how we got here.

Commerce began as a one-to-one relationship between buyer and seller — trading a goat for a haircut, a rug for a chicken. The Industrial Revolution enabled mass production of products, removing any connection to the seller. The emphasis was on the product, and the business owner's primary focus was on making affordable products.

Benefiting from systems innovation and mass distribution honed over previous decades, the Internet Age shifted the emphasis off products and onto people. The prominent focus was on market reach — in fact, in many respects, the product didn't matter.

> In the New Economy we've come full circle with a twist. We are returning to the direct association with the seller, re-establishing the ancient one-on-one relationship, although it's not just with one person...it's with many consumers through the Age of Social Media.

And not just any consumers, either, but those people who best align with what the business is selling. Trying to be all things to all people is a guaranteed strategy for failure.

BRAND RULE 3:
BE PREPARED TO DELIVER THE WHOLE MEAL

For decades, marketers have been told to "sell the sizzle, not the steak." This comes from the glittery golden age of advertising with its flashy cars, celebrity endorsements, glamour and glitz galore. Underneath, the product often disappointed when the excitement wore off, creating a whole generation of consumers who have grown wary of "flash." In short, companies failed to create value in the product, only the "promise" of it via the advertising.

Disillusioned consumers wary of being disappointed by "the sizzle" are now demanding the steak, three side dishes, and dessert, and want to know everything about the meal including where it came from and why it exists...PLUS a guarantee.

> It can't just smell like coffee and come in a pretty cup; if you want to charge five bucks for a cup, it better be great coffee, in a useful cup, delivered with a smile, piping hot, in an environment that creates a memorable experience. Starbucks understands this.

BRAND RULE 4:
IT HAS TO BE REAL

Modern consumers can smell when something's not real. The sizzling smokescreen doesn't work anymore — actually, it never did long-term. In the New Economy, people are more discerning regarding how to spend their money. That means, you — and your product — need to establish a connection with your customers that wins their loyalty and keeps them coming back. They need to trust in the promise of a good brand — that it offers them real connection and value for their time and money.

BRAND RULE 5:
NEEDS TO BE MORE

We all want to feel that we have given our money and our loyalty to something worthwhile. The fly-by-night marketer earns our contempt because he has stolen our trust along with our cash. Your brand must stand for something, whether it answers a need in our society, helps the environment, or is simply good clean fun. Every single thing you do builds a brand impression in the minds of your customers, from the quality of the products to the outlets you choose to sell them.

A brand done well is rooted deep inside the founder. It engages people and keeps them coming back with a personal attachment to your brand: your products or services.

> **Everyone who comes in contact with your brand should get from it a clear understanding of what you stand for—your culture, your values, your brand soul...the things you are passionate about solving.**

In the New Economy, a small business can literally change the world, by providing independence for its owner and jobs for others, money for charitable causes, and new products to shape the world around us. All of that is tied directly to the brand and its DNA, because it is the brand that people ultimately trust—and in the New Economy, that spells the difference between a vital, thriving business, and one that is perpetually skating on the edge and never understanding why.

By following these undeniable rules, you can be sure that you'll have what it takes to not only survive in the coming age of business, you will thrive.

NEXT STEPS

Have a look at BrandU®, the world's only process-based, integral approach to business creation that guides small business owners and entrepreneurs around the world to grow from idea to brand to consistent sales in the market:

www.brandubiz180.com

www.facebook.com/brandu

For nearly a decade, BrandU®, a revolutionary three-stage business development system, often dubbed the "E-myth® for a new generation of business" has been guiding thousands of entrepreneurs and small business owners to grow beyond the confusion of possibility to the power of extreme clarity—from idea to their million dollar brand.

Want to learn how companies like Virgin, Apple and Disney create loyal customers for life? Start growing your brand for FREE with the CD "7 Secrets to Today's Top-earning Brands." Get your instant download TODAY at:

www.BrandU.com/avins

BUSINESS GROWTH

MICHELLE
CLARKE

Founder of Talent Dynamics in 2010 with Roger James Hamilton. Talent Dynamics is an extension of Wealth Dynamics, created specifically for corporates and large teams, and was recognised as a finalist in the highly coveted BIBA New Business of the Year awards.

Michelle has led large corporate teams, helped build small businesses and establish global enterprises.
As former Head of Leadership Development for Retail at Marks & Spencer PLC she was responsible for the M&S move into Germany, developing the national leadership team for future expansion.

In 2006 she built her own business, to allowed her to combine he exceptional skills of speaking, writing and performance consulting by adapting Wealth Dynamics as the primary tool for facilitating team and individual business success in her customers' businesses.

Michelle gained significant experience as head of an internationa social entrepreneurs network for building global teams, and training and developing leaders in 22 countries and 55 cities around the world She also led a global transition · project which transformed and launched XL Nation in 25 countries.

She launched the charity StepUP Foundation in the UK in 2008 to give teenagers access to inspiring speakers and mentors and is involved regularly as a volunteer in the local community

TEAM SPORTS

I have long been a huge fan of Wealth Dynamics profiling –
I can't tell you the difference it made to the way I approach
my business once I understood my own profile.

I was introduced to Michelle's material again when we were
both speaking at the KPI weekend seminar in London. I sat
at the back of the room (one of the perks of all the
speaking I do is I get to hear all the other innovators at
these events!) and was completely bowled over to hear her
explain how, with Talent Dynamics, she has taken all of
these insights into the world of building high performance
teams... I just had to get her input into this book for
you – enjoy!

— *Paul Avins*

Did team sports frustrate you when you were growing up? They did me. It always seemed like the wrong people played in the wrong positions on the netball court. Who chose those positions? The team captain of course. And she often got it wrong.

Put people in a position to win

I could see what the problem was: the girl with the quickest turn of speed was wasted as goal keeper while the most popular girls got to be goal shooters. I remember we lost far more games than we won, and even then only because of the individual efforts of some exceptional players. I wondered then what our results might be if we all helped each other rather than busting a gut for personal glory in every match. We were only called a team because we were all wearing the same coloured kit.

Now that I run my own business I see many of the same basic mistakes with my clients' companies that I saw back then on the netball court – too many people stuck in the wrong roles or performing tasks in ways that conflict with their own natural approach.

Some time ago I figured that if people recognised how they approached problems and – just as crucially – how their colleagues approached those problems, how much better the business would function. If employees were allowed to perform their tasks, be creative and problem-solve in a way that suited their unique talents while simultaneously helping others in their team express themselves – what effect would that have on productivity? In other words, what if everybody played in their natural positions on the court? Imagine a team that rather than get in each other's way (do you recognise this yet?) they do all they can to enable other team members to reach their own goals.

Energy follows where attention goes!

Talent Dynamics calls this Flow. If you were to use a simple profiling tool that identified your strengths and those of the people around you, and you considered each day how you could help them reach their goals, your organisation would be close to reaching a state of flow. It would be like opening an irrigation gate onto a parched field. And you should expect a good crop next year. It also follows that your employees will have more fun, feel more valued, and contribute more to the organisation. That's when the exciting stuff begins to happen.

But flow is not enough by itself. Your business still has to make money. Your customers will only buy from you if they perceive your product or service as adding some value to their lives – and you must also leverage all your resources to support this through effective use of systems and people. Put the right people in the right place at the right time doing the right things and you shouldn't go far wrong. Easy. Well, no.

> It is much easier if your business has a strong purpose, or Why. It's the question that plagues every parent of a young child. Why? But that is also the question your employees may be asking about your business. Why am I coming to work? Why am I here? Why am I doing what I'm doing?

That question needs to be answered in the minds of all your team members before effective flow can take place. If the flow in your organisation gets blocked it may be because the Why needs to be revisited. It also helps if you create a culture that encourages collaboration over competition, where getting it right is more important than being right.

If you've read this far you deserve a nugget to take back to your business. This is the crucial bit, and it's a paradox: You can only get into flow by helping others get into flow. And that's a lot of flow. So once others are in flow and performing at their best you can focus on offering to them what you do best. Teams in flow do

BUSINESS GROWTH

not perform at exceptional levels by waking up in the morning and thinking 'How can I be more exceptional today?' but rather 'How can I help my team members be more exceptional?' Adopt this approach and you will start to view your colleagues in surprising new ways. And if the system is working you should now have a team of people around you thinking about you in surprising new ways. That's exciting. That's a reason to get up in the morning.

This concept is worth repeating:

> **Pooling resources will help your team work towards getting it right rather than individuals competing to be right.**

Whatever results you achieve in your team today – the financial returns, the quality of production, the level of service – will come as a direct result of the planning you did as a team yesterday. If you want to get a different result, you need to get a different plan. Create an amazing plan and you're more likely to get amazing results. My team at Talent Dynamics take out two or three days every six months to realign our strategy and embed the business goals. This is time well spent as our increased profitability clearly shows.

Having said that, success in the real world rarely come as easily as they make out in business books. My company, Talents Dynamics, is no different. But if we have setbacks we don't pretend they didn't happen. We get naked. By that I mean we openly share the business results, our individual performance, the sales targets we missed, the failed promotions and all the other disappointments in order to air the built-up frustrations with utter transparency. If your team is in flow they will apply solutions to these problems that make greater use of their talents – and help others to access theirs. This will also strengthen commitment to the team, which benefits everybody.

And unlike that netball team of mine that never reached its potential, with the far-reaching concept of flow in your toolkit your business now has the means to set out on a different path: the one where every member of your team not only wears the same coloured kit but also plays for each other and achieves the success you deserve.

NEXT STEPS

Take a Talent Dynamics Profile test, the first step to identifying your natural talent and the easiest way to get into flow.

You may have completed some kind of profiling test before that 'discovered' things you already knew about yourself - Extroverted or Introverted, Big Picture or Detail Orientated? Interesting yes, but how did it make a difference to your business?

Talent Dynamics is the only profiling test that tells you exactly what strategy you should follow to create greater flow in your life, your team and your business.

Using this special link, you can access two profiles for the price of one at:

www.tdprofiletest.com/paul-avins-book-offer/

and get into flow straight away.

I look forward to sharing a flow-filled journey with you.

BUSINESS GROWTH

ALAN FRENCH

His career started as an automotive engineer developing engines for Piaggio, Bentley & Scania.

In a number of senior manufacturing roles he managed new plant installations around the world for companies such as John Deere, Ford, & Mercedes Benz.

Alan started a new service business in Lucas Industries, where he grew the business to over £5M in three years.

He then went on to manage a niche consulting company in the UK providing operational change support to over 60 small, medium and large companies such as Rolls-Royce, Nokia, and Unilever, until it was sold in 2009. Alan has over 25 years line management and business growth experience in over 30 countries worldwide. Alan now mentors leaders, managers and teams in growing product & service companies.

Married with two fabulous children, he became part of a team that walked across the Arctic Ocean to the Geographical North Pole to raise over £250k for charity.

Alan is currently growing three new enterprises including the Business Wealth Club in St Albans. "My goal as a coach and mentor is to get local business owners and their teams excited about the business and its future. To do this I bring energy, enthusiasm and practical, relevant ways to accelerate sales, profits and value."

AN EXPEDITION INTO LEADERSHIP

When I first met Alan it was clear he was a true Business Adventurer! His track record of success speaks for itself, and it impressed me, but so did his desire to be a team player, not just a Leader. He wants to contribute to his clients, his community and to the success of his fellow Mentors.

His mechanical approach to systems and business has already helped drive us forward, and keep us on our toes, although we start to get worried when he brings up his next expedition that he might ask us to go!

— *Paul Avins*

> **Growing a business in today's harsh environment requires strong leadership; leadership in the market place, product and service leadership, in team working and in partnering with others.**
>
> **Someone has to show the way, inspire others to follow and to set the standards of behaviour for a Business to succeed.**

I have made many journeys in my life, both physically and mentally in setting up and growing businesses. Journeys that have required me to set direction, inspire others and act as an appropriate Role Model, Mentor and Coach.

Leadership is about serving others!

As Lao Tzu said, "in order to lead, one must follow." The journey that ultimately taught me this lesson was one to the Geographic North Pole with seven other business leaders...

The journey starts in a pub in Warwickshire in 2004 in which we talked about our next boys' trip away. Was it to be Golf, Skiing, or climbing Killy? Then my buddy Pete Goss, well known expedition leader and sailor suggested trekking to the North Pole! We immediately thought he'd lost the plot but the steely look from this ex-Marine made it perfectly clear he was serious. After several pints of Spitfire and naïve bravado, a collective commitment was made.

What was interesting about this commitment was that it felt right. Our hearts had ruled our heads. We knew nothing of the challenge that laid ahead, the logistics, the politics or just how cold it was going to be! Had we really thought it through, we'd never had done it. This was a big "Note to Self" for all of us. In business, we tended to "over think" things. Reducing risk and project planning before we agreed a goal. This time it was different, and it felt good. The goal, walking unsupported to the Geographic North Pole, came first. We planned to succeed. No "seeing if it can be done." Planning was not a decision making tool but a success guarantee.

Sat at the computer next morning, I realized what I had let myself in for. My Google research was not exactly selling the trip. We had chosen one of six North Poles (if you include Father Christmas's crib) as a destination, the Geographic North Pole, the axis the world rotates about, the most northerly point on the planet. Minus 25 degrees Celcius without wind chill. Minus 60 degrees with. Ice floes and 18,000 feet of Arctic Ocean to walk precariously across, pulling pulks that contained our food and shelter.

Few others had achieved the goal. Fortunately, Pete knew Alan Chambers who had become the first British Man to walk unsupported from Russia to the North Pole in 2000. Alan was to become our valued coach and mentor, something I advocate strongly in business. Yes, we might have managed to succeed without his help, but boy did he shortcut our preparation and achievements.

Now, the more I found out about the pole, the journey and the challenge, the more I was inspired. My idle moments had me daydreaming about the journey and reaching the pole.

> Never before had I been inspired so intimately. I had internalised the goal to the point that I was so certain of success that even the negative people around me started to believe. That for me was the essence of leadership – I had inspired others with my enthusiasm, energy and my unequivocal belief.

First, I needed to get fit and learn the skills required for the journey. I see the same need in business today. Training for fitness and survival were essential. I took it seriously and got out daily to drag my truck tyres around the local parks and beaches in an effort to simulate pulling a pulk across the ice. Many a raised eyebrow was encountered. It all helped to raise awareness of my journey, which I later monetised for charity.

I call that Marketing!

It was now March 2005. So far it had been easy. Some 4,500km from the pole, in an environment that was familiar to me, getting fit and learning new skills was second nature. Now was the time to apply all the learning in the hostile environment they call the Arctic.

To our dismay, our first attempt had to be abandoned after the Russians, who control the logistics on the polar ice cap, decided for political reasons to withdraw their rescue services. The window of 6 weeks in which attempts can be made was lost. We were devastated. All that preparation and investment financially, physically and emotionally wasted.

> **When you come to think of it, so many times in Business outside influences can impact your plans. It may be the Government, suppliers or even Banks - our goal was so strong that we vowed to return in 2006 and conquer all... and you must to.**

March 2006 saw less ice than the previous year. Some argued the effects of global warming. But the logistics worked this time. We got to start our journey for real. When the rattling Russian helicopter dropped us off, there was a real sense of euphoria. Just getting to the start line was a massive achievement. In my experience most Business Owners celebrate the launch of a new product or service, without recognizing the huge amount of effort and a little bit of luck that is expended in getting there. Celebration is something we don't do enough of in business.

> As we started in near "white out" conditions, I remember thinking about those days in business where we have doubts about reaching the goal - days when gut feel, vision and the odd measure of effort were all you could go on. I guessed it was about faith; faith in the plan, your team mates and Mother Nature.

As the days froze by, the icy routines of making breakfast, preparing the days' food and drink, breaking camp, ablutions, walking, making camp and cooking dinner eventually became second nature. It was a struggle to start with, mainly because everything had to be done against the clock. Taking your time in this hostile environment could not be afforded. Once learnt and executed without thinking, the team started to relax. Good old military training in action.

What I didn't expect was the comfort in the rhythm of the day and week.

> In my coaching I talk about setting up a business rhythm, Marketing Monday, Follow Up Friday etc. When something works you repeat it, you don't have to meddle with it constantly. When you have a team, a rhythm is essential to ensure progress and alignment. It promotes everyone to work together toward the goal.

With eight strong-minded business leaders, conflict was inevitable. The competition to ensure you weren't the weak link in the chain; the ideas for doing things differently and the difference in decision-making processes were all there to see on the ice. The harsh environment soon exposes differences but the power of humour and generosity got us through without a drop of blood being spilt.

For research purposes, I wore a Polar heart rate monitor. I was interested in how my body coped with the exercise. When walking on skis, you have to maintain a rhythm that doesn't make you sweat. Sweat would turn to ice and block the pores in your clothing. Apart from being very uncomfortable, you are more susceptible to hypothermia. I learnt a lot about my body on the trip. It became a study of heating and plumbing. My arms and legs would be "switched on" at certain temperatures and workloads. I burnt 7,800 calories a day; a lot of energy that had to be fuelled by food and drink. No wonder I lost 7kgs on the trip. That was in spite of eating copious amounts of chicken curry, porridge, chocolate, nuts and energy bars.

> **The lesson learnt; a leader needs to be fit for business and look after themselves constantly. After all, it's a marathon not a sprint and you need to be in it for the long term.**

Learn to enjoy the journey!

Managing the groups' physical energy was a skill we had to learn. Everyone, even the strongest amongst us had a bad day. A bad day meant redistributing the loads amongst the pulks. We had to learn when to stop and set up camp, knowing that this additional energy was required at the end of the day. We became expert at spotting the signs of people struggling and offering help in a matter of fact way, a skill I still often use with members of my Business Wealth Club.

Managing the groups' psychological energy was harder. There were days when we ended up further away from the pole than when we started 12 hours earlier. The ice floes could be wicked. It reminded me of those days at work where one seems to take one step forward and many steps backwards. We had to console ourselves that without the days' effort, we'd be many more miles adrift. I guess you could call it "always looking for the positive".

Finally on the 26th April 2006, we reached our goal; 90 degrees North. The very top of the world where every direction is South. The emotion that overcame us all was a shock. Grown men in tears of joy. We had achieved what some said was impossible. Our physical and mental investments had just paid dividends and victory was ours!

It's fun to do the impossible

To celebrate, we cooked bacon rolls. The taste was fantastic. Then came the toughest part of the whole trek. Mother Nature threw everything at us at a time when we had run out of fuel and food. It was bitterly cold with temperatures exceeding -60 degrees C.

We all learnt many lessons on this journey. However, the lessons of leadership in the Arctic echo in my mind everyday in business, and I've taught them to many of my Coaching clients over the years.

I hope they serve you on your expedition in Business as well as they have me...

NEXT STEPS

To down load one months FREE Membership to Alan's club - or to come and meet him in person, visit:

www.stalbans-businesswealthclub.co.uk

www.facebook.com/alanfrench61

BUSINESS GROWTH

ANDREW
GRIFFITHS

Andrew Griffiths is a man on a mission. He is passionate about helping people to achieve their dreams, no matter how big or bold they may be.

Acknowledged as Australia's #1 Small Business Author, Andrew has eleven books that are now sold in over fifty countries. His bestselling books take complex ideas and make them profoundly practical and simple. The fact that Andrew is published by two of the world's best publishers, Allen & Unwin and Simon & Schuster is further testament to the extraordinary insights that Andrew provides.

Andrew's latest book, *The BIG BOOK of Small Business*, is a culmination of his extensive work to date in the Small Business arena. At the same time, Andrew is promoting his concept of being a ONE PERCENTER – those one in a hundred businesses that just get it right. Who are they and how do they do it?

Andrew has taken tragedy in his life and turned it into triumph and he shares these experiences and so much more to inspire, energise and enthuse everyone he meets. He is inspiring and engaging but most importantly he is real, raw and extremely relevant in today's world.

WELCOME TO THE AGE OF THE ENTREPRENEUR

Andrew and I flew from opposite sides of the globe to attend the 4 day long Experts Academy workshop with Brendon Bruchard in 2010. As soon as we met I knew we had a connection and a shared passion for helping Entrepreneur's succeed, we had just been working in different hemispheres! I knew then that I wanted to get him involved in the first project where there was an opportunity, so I'm excited to have a Best Selling Author from Down Under in the book.

— *Paul Avins*

> I believe that we are well and truly living in the Age of the Entrepreneur and it is only just getting started. Many of the older barriers that stopped people from starting their own business are no longer relevant.

I love Thursday mornings because it's when I get my weekly newsletter from a website called *Springwise*. Now, what on earth could this email contain that could get someone like me so excited? Well it showcases what smart entrepreneurs are doing around the world and it blows my socks off every time I read it.

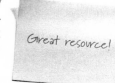

Great resource!

For starters it has never been cheaper to open a business. You don't need to have a shop, cars, trucks, big advertising campaigns or hundreds of staff. All you need is a good idea and the smarts to know how to outsource the skills and expertise that you need.

Today you don't even need to leave your job. In the olden days, that is BG (Before Google), we had to make a decision, work for someone or have our own business, rarely could you do both.

I have personally met people who generate between five and ten million dollars per year, from a room in their house, with one full time employee. Now, the profit margin with this kind of business is exceptionally high and I know that not every business will fit into this category, in fact the vast majority won't. But I have also met thousands of people who have started a business to supplement their income and they are making a few hundred dollars a week, and that means a huge amount to them. It is the difference between a private and public school, or a holiday every year, or getting their own home.

What does this mean for the rest of us, those of us who have been in a business for a while?

Well for starters if we thought business was competitive before, hang onto your hats because we are about to learn the true meaning of the word.

Secondly we need to learn from these new entrepreneurs. They are entering the business world without most of the preconceptions that we have. For example they don't think running a business should be about sacrifice with little return. They think it should be about making as much money as you need and having a blast doing it.

A really big issue facing many older entrepreneurs is their struggle to adapt. These "old dogs" have to learn new tricks and I certainly include myself in this category. I seem to be spending more time presenting to rooms full of people who have been incredibly successful in the past, but now they are really struggling to find their way into the new world, particularly the online environment.

> **Our history is no longer enough to keep our customers coming back. They will be loyal, to a point, but if the competitor up the road is better at engaging with our customers through smarter communication, more creative offerings and innovative ways of doing business, they will go to them in droves.**

Last but not least (and believe me I could write a book about this entire subject), we need to run our businesses with a level of integrity that is beyond question. Consumers want to know that they are dealing with an ethical and honest organisation, regardless of its size. The reality is that big is no longer better and there is a worldwide mistrust of "big" that is gaining momentum. It doesn't take long to figure out whom to blame for this, just think back to a few front pages over the past two years.

BUSINESS GROWTH

SO WHERE TO FROM HERE?

I honestly don't think there has ever been a better time to have your own business. The playing field is as level as it will ever be and consumers are as open-minded as they will ever be. My advice is to go for it, give it all you have.

But be warned – the world is changing and how we do business needs to change accordingly. Tomorrow's successful businesses will be those who have mastered the art of evolution, for them the Age of the Entrepreneur will be an incredible time.

Take Note!

For those who don't evolve, the Age of the Entrepreneur will be much tougher.

Like many of the trends that we are seeing around the world, gaps are appearing. The gap between the wealthy and the poor is getting bigger. The gap between those that embrace technology and those that are scared of it is getting bigger. This concept will certainly be applied to the entrepreneurial world. There are those who get it and those that don't, and that is the growing gap.

No matter how uncomfortable it may make us, we need to be on the side of the gap that get's it. But the really good news is that once you make the decision to really embrace evolution in your business, you will suddenly notice all of the other businesses out there that are doing the same. And you will realise you are not alone, instead you are part of a dynamic, energetic and creative group that realizes the full potential of the entrepreneurial world now and in the coming years. So clearly, the pay off is big.

Everyone wants to be associated with a really dynamic, energetic and creative business. That means staff are lining up to join these businesses – and good staff. Suppliers want to be involved with these businesses and they are willing to do whatever they can to be a part of these showcase businesses. And most importantly of all, customers want to buy from businesses like this. Not once, but for a long time. The ultimate example of this entire concept has to be the Apple Corporation. Everyone wants to be a part of this company – from staff to investors and enough customers to sell a $1 Billion USD a week worth of cool stuff.

For me, I see the line in the sand. Now is the time that we as entrepreneurs need to wake up, step up and skill up and get ready to build incredible businesses in the years ahead. It will be a roller coaster road, but lets be honest, that is what most of us love the most. Welcome to the AGE of the ENTREPRENEUR.

NEXT STEPS

Visit:

www.ultimatesmallbusinesssuccesspackage.com

to find out about Andrew's incredible special offer. This really is the Ultimate Small Business Package, which is shipped anywhere in the world. It includes a pile of books, CD's, DVD's and a 12 month subscription to the Small Business Academy of Success.

Check this out NOW.

BUSINESS GROWTH

THESE TWO SKILLS WILL BE AT THE HEART OF YOUR SUCCESS AS A BUSINESS OWNER OR ENTREPRENEUR, THEY ARE THE FUEL THE DRIVES YOUR BUSINESS GROWTH...

SALES
MARK

&
ETING

LEIGH ASHTON

Leigh is an author, speaker, trainer and coach... and the founder of The Sales Consultancy.

Leigh specialises in helping people incorporate psychology alongside technical selling skills – leading to positive changes in attitude, approach and sales results. It was early in her 28 year sales career, she became increasingly frustrated by the inconsistent performance of her sales team and was inspired to find out why this happens... and crucially how to fix it. What she discovered was that what goes on inside a person's head has the biggest impact on whether they achieve sales success or not.

In 1996 Leigh formed The Sales Consultancy and since then has trained thousands of sales people. Her findings remain consistent; even when outwardly confident, sales people often lack the inner confidence and practical strategies to achieve great sales on a consistent basis.

Working with Business Owners, Directors, Managers and Sales Teams to identify and eliminate their own psychological barriers & limiting beliefs... and the reasons or excuses they use to rationalise their lack of consistently great sales. Leigh is known for increasing sales from 20% to over 100% and leaves people feeling inspired and motivated to take massive action! See www.sales-consultancy.com

THE NEW INGREDIENTS OF
SALES
SUCCESS

I met Leigh for a second time when I was guest speaker at a KPI Seminar on using Joint Ventures and Partnerships to grow your business. We had met before at an event but this time we connected and I realised here was a lady with a unique perspective on the world of sales in the new economy. She asked me to review her first book *iSell*, which it was my pleasure to do. I was only half way through when I decided to ask her to contribute her perspective to this book. You'll be glad I did.

— *Paul Avins*

> Sales professionals and business owners constantly ask me what the most important factor is when it comes to great sales results.
>
> That's like asking what the most important ingredient is when baking a cake!
>
> If you don't have all the ingredients...you end up with something else.

Interestingly, you can have all the ingredients and still not have the cake. Too much flour, too little butter, not enough sugar or eggs means you don't get what you want.

This is also true in sales. Too much of some activity and too little of something else could seriously limit your success. Especially in times of change... and there sure has been plenty of that in the last few years.

OUT: Heavy handed pressure sales techniques, sales scripts, 'gift of the gab' sales winners, death by PowerPoint, 'all talking and no listening' pitches.

IN: Building genuine rapport, integrity and trust, long term win/win relationships and a positive consultative approach.

Technology is changing fast, attitudes are changing, and the selling arena is changing. There's social change... economic change... environmental change. Changes are changing!

You need to be one step ahead at all times if you're to achieve sales success, which is why you are reading this book!

In sales there's a greater emphasis on psychology than ever before, both to understand yourself and your clients! What goes on inside your head will have the biggest impact on your sales success.

When working with people that are not getting the sales results they want I find some common themes playing out.

The 3 things that will seriously impact your sales results are:

1. *What you believe*

2. *Who or what is to blame*

3. *How you get into rapport*

I 100% agree!

WHAT YOU BELIEVE

Your beliefs along with your values are core to who you are. You will defend them with passion. For you, they are ultimate truths.

When your beliefs are positive like... the world is full of opportunities, there are people spending money out there, I am a great sales person... they will empower you. Give you confidence. Raise your self esteem. Keep you motivated.

You also have other beliefs. The ones that make you feel un-resourceful. These could be... I'm not very good with those types of people, I can't make my first call till I've had a coffee, I don't think I can do that... or similar. These are limiting beliefs and they will stop you getting the sales you want.

If you're not getting great sales results, limiting beliefs will be at play.

Limiting beliefs are often deep rooted and you may not even know that they are lingering in your unconscious. The good news is that you can actually do something about them once you become aware of what they are.

An easy way to do this is to find yourself a quiet space, take some paper and give yourself plenty of time.

SALES & MARKETING

> Make a list of all the things that you either don't do well or avoid altogether. Once you have your list ask yourself for each one... *What stops me doing this?* Write down everything that pops into your head...even if it doesn't quite make sense. Keep writing until there's absolutely nothing left to say.

Stop right now and do this exercise – take action!

Go through what you've written and highlight all the negative things you say about yourself. You now have a list of limiting beliefs that you can now tackle.

Most limiting beliefs are built on assumption rather than fact and a very simple approach to eliminating them is to find 3 examples where you have exhibited the opposite behaviour to your limiting belief. For example... if your limiting belief is that you are not very good at follow up calls then come up with 3 examples where you made great follow up calls.

Without exception, all the sales professionals and business owners I work with always come up with at least 3 examples.

Because you accept your beliefs as ultimate truths you only remember the occasions that support your beliefs. Focus on what you do well and remember that when something doesn't go well... you learn from it.

WHO OR WHAT IS TO BLAME

How often do you catch yourself saying things like... my sales results are not great because the economy is down or because budgets are frozen or because people are keeping hold of their money?

Because, because, because means it's not your fault. You can't help it. It's out of your control. As soon as you start believing your own reasons and excuses for lack of results you are doomed! In all cases of poor performance this pattern is at play.

You can convince yourself that you're trying really hard but the reality is that this thinking will stop you giving 100%... why would you, with all these outside forces to contend with. It also relinquishes any responsibility to do something about it.

This renders you a victim... and victims don't make sales.

Every time you hear yourself come up with an excuse for lack of results answer the following question:

> **OK... so if all that is true...what are you going to do to counteract it and get the sales you want?**

I love this section!

Taking action gives you back control and ultimately generates options for overcoming your sales challenges.

HOW YOU GET INTO RAPPORT

There's no mystery to rapport. It's the very natural result of people really connecting.

In sales it's absolutely crucial. The ability to get into deep levels of rapport is what makes the difference between an OK sales person and an amazing one.

Matching and mirroring your clients physiology, their voice patterns and the language they use will really allow them to feel comfortable and at ease to talk freely. Be sure to use lots of good open questions to encourage dialogue. It's also really important to model their map of the world. Let me explain.

The map according to me, Leigh Ashton has been created from the moment I was born to this very day. All the people I've come into contact with, the experiences I've had, the reactions, significant emotional events... in fact everything that has occurred in my life. It's impossible for two people to have the exact same experiences in life and therefore impossible for people to have the same map of the world.

This is really important, so take note.

- When you communicate with anyone you absolutely must get into their map of the world to get deep levels of rapport.

- You need deep levels of rapport to uncover their true thinking. You need their true thinking to know if you can help them.

- You need to absolutely know that you can help them to create a mutually beneficial long lasting business relationship.

An indication that you are in the other person's map of the world is that you will be using *you* language. Every time you say 'we' you are in your map. For example rather than 'we offer you....' it's more effective to say 'you will get....' Other than asking open questions you should be doing little of the talking.

Find out about their map of the world, what's important to them, what problems they have and what they want to achieve... then and only then can you add value. Leave sales pitches to the sales talkers and make sure you become a listener and fixer.

TIME FOR ACTION

Now that you have some ingredients to use in your sales recipe... what are you going to do next?

How are you going to ensure you use what you have learned to create more sales?

It's all about action. Knowing and doing are two different things.

So what are your three priority actions that you're going to take as a result of reading this chapter?

1. ....

....

2. ....

....

3. ....

....

Now that you have some action points, put time in your diary to do them. Think about how you can make sure these happen... Do you need an accountability buddy? Do you need inspiring images around you to keep you on track? Maybe it's something else for you. Whatever you need to make these happen... do it!

NEXT STEPS

Spend time thinking about the things that could get in the way of you completing these actions. What do you need to do to counteract these potential pitfalls? What's your contingency plan?

With that in place, go do them as quickly as you can...anytime NOW would be good.

Get Leigh's new book - iSell, on Amazon now.

www.sales-consultancy.com

SALES & MARKETING

STEVE
BROOKS

Selling has always been Steve's true vocation, and it was early on in his career that he realised he had a natural flair for doing a deal.

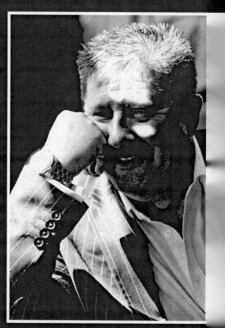

Within 12 months of being recruited to a position which would see Steve pull all his retail and selling skills together, Steve had purchased the business out right. He went on to create and sell several companies within what has become his area of expertise, commercialisation.

Now a serial Entrepreneur, Steve has over 30 years experience working in the UK retail & shopping centre industry, specifically in generating income in shopping centres around 3rd party activity in mall areas – i.e product demonstrations, kiosk operations, photo booths and short term pop up retail businesses. He is a well-respected partner in many of the major shopping centres across the UK including Lakeside, Bluewater and Westfield's – as well as centres in Dubai, Jordan and Abu Dhabi. His clients have included Xerox T-Mobile, Superdrug, Arabian Oud and BT.

Steve's focus has always been helping businesses grow, through the medium of face-to-face marketing in shopping centres "Helping business big and small to "get new customers". He is the author of the book *Make an Exhibition of Yourself – The Secrets of Success in Shopping Centre Sales.*

THE HIDDEN SOURCE OF NEW CUSTOMERS

I first met Steve at the *Make it Big Seminar* in London in 2010 where I was speaking.

Having bought my products and devoured and applied learnings from my book, Business SOS, he asked me to Coach him to take his business forward.

What initially impressed me about Steve was his determination to succeed and his creativity in solving problems for his clients and his own businesses (at that time he owned five!). The fact that he also owned an IT company dedicated to getting more Apple computers into businesses was a nice added bonus for me. Especially when the new models launched!

What surprised me about his business was how unknown it was and yet how simple, powerful and profitable it was to be one of his clients who knew about this little hidden gem of a business model.

Warning! His strategies are a little off the wall, some would even say crazy but they are used by companies like Sky TV, BT and T-Mobile as well as thousands of small businesses and start-ups.

If you want an underground sales and marketing maverick – he's your man!

— *Paul Avins*

> If your business has a retail offering or could have, and you want to test a retail concept or simply need to generate leads for your sales team - then I'm about to open the door to a new and exciting world for you.

There is so much online based information in this book, but if you're looking for unconventional ideas and information or a way to access hidden, pre-qualified and largely forgotten new customers then perhaps this chapter is for you.

What am I talking about? Well, using pop-up retail outlets and working in shopping centres, now I bet that took you by surprise.

Let me start by busting the No1 myth about using a shopping centre: "It's going to cost me a fortune!". People say to me all the time...the truth is it's just not as expensive as you might think.

Yes that's right it's not as expensive as you might think, in fact I'll bet when I tell you later on just how low the actual figure is you'll be shocked.

So, if you do have a retail business, idea or concept what are the key factors you need to consider?

THE HIDDEN SOURCE OF NEW CUSTOMERS

Firstly, you'll need to connect with your customers as most of them are on their way to somewhere else and not looking for you.

Secondly, you'll need to have a great attention grabbing proposition or product.

> **Finally you MUST offer amazing customer service as you are dealing with the public in full view of other potential customers and anything less will just not cut it. In reality if you have the last two wrong then the first makes no difference at all.**

'WOW' service builds big brands

Placing your business in a shopping mall gives you such a competitive advantage, but you may not even realise the opportunity you are being given. For example, being on the mall walkways means you don't have to spend your budget on expensive shop fittings, you don't have to dress windows, light the store to be inviting, or invest thousands in good signage to get people into your shop and over the threshold.

The result?

Your marketing budget can be used to deliver huge value to your business, not on fixed costs or fittings for your landlord.

Shopping centres spend millions of pounds every year attracting their customers, who often come for a day out with cash in their pocket.

What does this mean for you? Well simply put, you don't have to! You also don't have to provide parking for your customers, they already did that, you may not even need to buy a stand to run your business from as they have provided that too. So very low start up costs for a new business idea, or market test of a new product.

Lets look at some of this in more detail...

> When I speak to potential users of shopping centres the objections I hear time after time is "oh no I can't afford it" …. Hold the front page … you can. Believe it or not you can get in to some centres for as little as £150.00 per week. Yes that's right!

There are locations out there that are within even the most modest of budgets. The next thing always seems to be "Oh I can't commit long term". Well good news here as well – you don't have too; you can book a location for just a week, yes, that's right just a week. In fact some centres will let you do just a weekend – show me another business model that gives you that kind of flexibility.

SO WHAT ARE YOU GETTING FOR YOUR MONEY?

It varies from location to location, some offer just the space, I will talk about this later in the chapter. Some will provide Retail Merchandise Units or RMUs. These are units the centre has invested in that offer power, light and security for you to market your products from.

Think of them as a very modern indoor market stall, only far more attractive and in a warm, bright, secure and customer focused location.

You are also in full view of everyone who walks through the centre, you're on show the whole time and hey, you didn't have to spend any money to attract them either.

This isn't a license to print money. You still have to market the problem you solve. Go the extra mile and have a value for money product backed by outstanding customer service. You can't have your staff sitting reading a paper or drinking a coffee, they need to engage everyone who shows an interest without being intrusive.

If the centre does not have any RMUs, then you will need to provide your own stand. Each centre has its own criteria for this, but as sales professionals you will want to present your business in the best possible light.

A FEW HINTS FOR BOTH RMUS AND YOUR OWN STANDS WOULD BE:

- Don't have any hand written signage – it looks tacky and unprofessional

- Make sure you're open the whole time the centre is trading after all that is what you're paying for

- Make sure your products are priced clearly; we have all become very sophisticated in our shopping habits

- Offer great customer service, and deliver it!

If you are looking to generate leads then you will need an attractive and exciting pop-up stand. You can buy these from so many places now the list would just go on and on.

Just remember, don't make them too text heavy. Have a clear call to action, oh and please, please, please don't forget to put your contact details on it. Yes I have seen banners where people have forgotten to put any contact details on. Unbelievable!

Crazy but True!

Don't be pushy on the stand either, centres don't like it and surprise surprise... nor will your potential customers. I have seen so many companies fail through having aggressive staff manning their promotions.

SALES & MARKETING

> Remember people don't like to be sold to but they love to be engaged, educated and entertained.

You will need Public Liability Insurance (PLI) – the average is around £5 Million indemnity. Your business insurance broker will be able to assist you with this.

Finding the right location can be a minefield and where do you start? There are a number of potential routes you can follow. Spend hours calling centres, or visiting them, use your own marketing agency to source a venue or use a specialist agency. These can be found on any Google search using key words like shopping centre promotions, you can also visit www.mall-services.com. If you're looking for a stand or banner then why not visit www.blueprintprojects.co.uk.

We have only scratched the service here about a fantastic economical and effective way to start, grow or test your business so I am going to make you, the reader, an offer you can't refuse.

Every business needs an edge and using a shopping centre could be the one for you.

NEXT STEPS

If you would like to find out more about putting your business in front of your next customer then I will give you a free day's consultancy to explore ways in which you can use shopping centres to grow your business and increase your profits, but that's not all, we will give you 10% off your first booking at a centre when you book through Mall-Services.com, oh and at least a 10% discount on any pop up banners, or kiosks you might need to get you started, and finally a free copy of my own book 'Make an Exhibition of Yourself – the Secrets of Success in Shopping Centre Sales.'

steve@mall-services.com, call: 01376-565430 Ext 231

www.mall-services.com

www.twitter.com/stephenabrooks

SALES & MARKETING

BERNIE
DE SOUZA

Bernie De Souza is a family man with 4 children, 3 boys and 1 girl; he is a cricket lover and playing member of the Marylebone Cricket Club.

He is a leading authority in human behaviour with 20 years' experience TV and BBC 5 Live interviews have made him a sought after international motivational keynote speaker.

He has spoken in over 40 different countries and is credited with helping professionals at the top of their profession to build trust and rapport amongst colleagues and clients, improve their presentation skills and harmonise their teams.

His bestselling book Your Success is hidden in Your Daily Routine and various training products have helped thousands of people around the World to improve their results, increase their confidence and increase their income. See www.berniedesouza.com

THE 15 MAGIC WORDS TO HELP YOU GET MORE CLIENTS, MORE EASILY WITHOUT EVEN SELLING

The first time I saw Bernie was from the back of Wembley Conference Centre where he was in front of 10,000 people, being recognised on Stage as a Successful Young Entrepreneur. I was blown away with his hunger to learn and his ability to take Massive Action to get the results he wanted. Our paths crossed again several years ago, this time as speakers at the same event and we swapped cards and kept in touch. I've been impressed by the growth in him as a speaker and performance coach and the results he's helped his high profile clients achieve. I'm excited to have him share his wisdom with you here...

— *Paul Avins*

> When I am asked to do public speaking and training, the first skill people want to learn is how to make their presentation successful, without becoming a "hard core" pushy salesperson.

I use this simple system in my networking business and in my conventional businesses. I first learnt of this method in Canada, but recently revisited a similar model from business strategist, Peter Thomson (also in this book).

See, even the top guys never stop learning!

Use of the 15 magic words pro-active agenda will separate you from your competition. You will gain immediate rapport, credibility and the attention of everyone at the meeting.

Here are six of the incredible benefits. You will:

1.   Look more professional

2.   Keep the meeting on track

3.   Bring the sale to a smooth conclusion

4.   Understand who has the buying power

5.   Increase your conversion rates and make more money

6.   Be organised and respectful of your client's time

As well as giving you these six powerful advantages, it also opens your client's mind so they buy into this process too.

This can be used in business-to-business meetings as well as business-to-consumer. So let's go through how we use this programme. Let's assume you have already made the appointment.

If you find it difficult to make appointments by phone visit:

www.berniedesouza.com/get-more-appointments-by-phone

You arrive at your prospect's office; maybe you are offered a coffee and a seat.

When you speak to people you must understand the importance of "rhythms of three". These are three benefits that you offer. They must be totally client-benefit focused; such as more clients, higher profits, lower costs. This takes the meeting away from the coffee and politely prepares for the magic words.

Let me give you an example of what to say before the magic words. This will help you reconfirm the amount of time allocated to the meeting. "So Dawn, from my understanding we have 45 minutes to discuss how we can help you get more clients, with bigger accounts and promote brand awareness, is this about right?" (Then pause)

Whoever mumbles, crumbles. The only answer you should get is "yes" as it is impossible to say "no" because it is what they want to talk about or blind bullets which are in their profession. I know what you are thinking now – what is a blind bullet? Blind bullets are general client benefits for example; my programme will help you get more clients, more easily and, more often.

These benefits do not give specific outcomes, but they are general benefits to the client.

Another example would be, let us say you are meeting a graphics designer. "So John, from my understanding we have about 40 minutes to discuss how we can help you get more clients, reduce advertising costs and increase sales to existing clients, is that about right?" (Then pause)

Assuming they said: "yes" you have now prepared them to receive the 15 magic words pro-active agenda.

So here goes; here are the 15 magic words to set the scene. There are reasons for choosing this particular order of words:

> *"So…..." "Here is our agenda. Is there anything you wish to add or is this OK?"* (Pass a copy of the agenda to the client.)

Whoever hears these 15 magic words will be thinking: "Wow this person is organised and considerate." They will appreciate this opening.

This definitely separates you from the competition. Now let's break these 15 magic words into groups.

STAGE ONE

The word *"So"* introduces the 15 magic words and is powerful in this context; it means you have something important to say. If you use the word *"So"* together with their name, as in *"So, John"* (then pause) it means that what you have to say is important and it is personal because you have used their name.

STAGE TWO

The first group of the 15 magic words: *"Here is our agenda."* This politely tells your client that you have been thinking about them, you have prepared for the meeting, and you take them seriously.

STAGE THREE

"Is there anything you wish to add?" This tells your client that, even though you have taken control of the meeting, you are flexible in that you have given them an opportunity to add something and you are not attempting to control the meeting completely; you are open to their suggestions. This also forces people to read the total agenda; again, it is a win-win position. You are opening their minds to make it easier to talk about your agenda.

STAGE FOUR

Next you give them the option to say "yes" by saying: *"or is this ok?"* This gives you permission to continue with the agenda. It is important that you pause after *"or is this ok?"* Again, after this pause, whoever mumbles, crumbles. Be patient and wait for the "yes".

Over the years in direct sales with consumers and in business-to-business meetings in almost every case the client says "yes" and we move on.

There is a special template to use for your agendas that guide the prospect through your selling process. The template includes areas to check the smooth process of point to point steps. This template is available with training material to help you get more clients more easily using these 15 magic words (without even selling) here is a link to a short video to explain this.

www.berniedesouza.com/15-magic-words.html

NEXT STEPS

If you would like a copy of a sample template that you can modify for your business, complete with an eight-page booklet with more detailed instructions, simply send an email to:

Bernie@berniedesouza.com

or call 07795 600700.

www.berniedesouza.com

NICK
GRIFFITH

Nick is highly regarded as one of UKs leading networkers, connectors and JV managers in the events industry. Recently, a passion for Marketing; Creating Events and Building Networks of the right 'high-level' people has seen Nick create JV Dinners – a networking and social event for business owners and list owners who can bring value to each other's businesses. Nick is someone who knows everyone who's worth knowing or he knows how to contact them.

He started his career in Management Consultancy after achieving a Masters from Imperial College in Mechanical Engineering back in 1999.

Nick has spent the last 5 years in events and marketing during which he has filled many rooms with thousands of attendees and has created speaker alliances that have generated many £millions. Nick has developed state-of-the-art copywriting skills and more recently he has also created a partnership to help other businesses successfully build and launch membership sites.

RAPPORT AND CONNECTION
FOR SUCCESSFUL
JOINT
VENTURES

I've known Nick in many different roles over the years. JV Manager for Dr Joanna Martin and Marcus de Maria. A Membership Site Facilitator, Business Owner and Creator of the JV Dinner Network. He is one of the best "Connectors" I have ever met. If I want to be introduced to somebody in the industry... then Nick is the first call I make. I've been attending his JV Dinners for some time now and have always made contacts that have taken my business forward..... including a number of people who you are learning from in this book!

— *Paul Avins*

> **95% of your peers and competitors are not doing what I describe here for successful Joint Ventures (JV). Sure you can swap business cards, ask for recommendations, go networking but what else could you be doing?**

Can you remember a time when you decided not to do business because you didn't have rapport with the person? I believe people do business with people who they have rapport and a connection with. If you want to expand your business through Joint Ventures, developing deeper rapport and connection with potential partners should be one of your top priorities.

Face-to-face networking is a great way of developing rapport but why bother with the hassle of travel, noisy bars and poor quality networking that are the feature of many networking events? (Excluding The Business Wealth Club of course!)

Answer: You start not to bother. So back in 2010 I decided to create my own more intimate 'high level' networking JV Dinner events.

Great distinction!

I believe in the adage 'It's not what you know, it's who you know' but I think there's more to it than that. It's not who you know but the level of rapport and connection you have with your contacts that will determine how much business gets done.

We all spend so much time and effort trying to go through the 'front door', we forget there are other ways to get people's attention, for example:

Over a number of days I sent a series of emails and text messages to a well-known Internet Marketeer asking if he was interested in doing a JV – no answer. On the last day I invited him to a JV Dinner – he replied within 30 minutes (I think you have to give before you can expect to receive.) I didn't force my JV idea on him at my JV Dinner; however I did book a time I could call the next day to follow up. Deal done!

HERE ARE SOME OTHER TRUE STORIES FROM THE PAST YEAR

Two business owners meet and see potential in Joint Venturing; they then spend the next 6 months exchanging emails and calls. It was only after a JV Dinner event where they met again and agreed the deal; this happened because they were in a relaxed, social environment where there was less selling pressure and they had time to build rapport and connect.

After a recent JV Dinner I suggested to my guests that they go and entertain their top clients. Shortly afterwards an experienced consultant visited his top client on the day they announced the bonuses for the year. It turned out he also qualified for a share – his reaction? He said I'm taking you all out for lunch, on me. Their response?

They signed him up for another year. Money well re-invested?

When was the last time you took your top 5 customers out for a high class social dinner and really talked to them? The topic of sales might not even come up. Use the face-to-face time to build rapport and connect with them as individuals.

Would you like some other tips that I've picked up after running high level JV Dinners for the past year? (You don't owe me anything – I'm giving these to you as a gift, in fact if you would like more tips on how to run a successful 'high level' networking event then please go to www.jvdinners.com/tips)

I gained my experience and my book of contacts through hard work crewing other speakers events, to being an affiliate for other Business Experts, to working as a full time JV manager. Some of my highlights include filling the first T. Harv Eker event in London's ExCeL and putting 500 people in Earls Court for Brian Tracy in 2010. When I attend events, instead of networking with the audience I networked with the promoters, the speakers and the main affiliates and I always asked the same thing – how can I help you?

Now I have a list of all the key promoters, speakers and business owners in the events industry.

SALES & MARKETING

Are there shortcuts for building rapport (which can take years)?

Yes and No – you can build rapport with one person, who in turn has rapport with many others.

People try and rush the rapport building process and jump straight into business. This is a mistake.

Once there is rapport and a connection:

- It's easier to do business together (any issues can be resolved)

- You're more likely to speak frequently and hence catch new opportunities earlier

- You're more likely to sign on-going/renewed business since you have made a personal connection

Keys for successful 'high level' networking events:

This is a golden checklist!

- The majority of people need to be like-minded and of a 'similar level'

- Always have some 'well known' names which act as social proof for others

- Be honest – there is no room for hype when you're talking to millionaires and people at the top

- Choose a venue and a location that reflects your business brand and the calibre of people who are attending

To recap, here are the main reasons I started JV Dinners:

- You will be amazed at how many new JV's are created by not discussing business – try it and see for yourself

- You can bring together a number of busy people on one day and create a 'win-win' environment – imagine how much time you would spend to meet every one of them individually?

- They are relatively low cost (private room hire in the best restaurants is free, so make use of it)

- They make you stand out from your competitors in a positive light

- Most people/businesses are too lazy or lack the imagination to take any action

- You can start today with an event of any size – even just 2 people

NEXT STEPS

Many of my guests have been to other networking events and left disappointed – there is no doubt there is a formula to getting it right. JV Dinners has this formula and is working to improve it each month. If you are interested in attending one of my monthly JV Dinners or getting help setting up your own, please go to:

www.jvdinners.com/tips *and register your details.*

SALES & MARKETING

DOUG HECKER

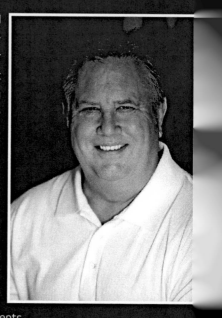

Doug Hecker is a goal driven and dedicated professional with 30+ years experience with a number of Fortune 500 multi-unit retail corporations including Conocophilips, 7-Eleven and Circle K convenience stores as well as owning his own retail supply and marketing companies.

He now uses his vast expertise in marketing, sales, management, and operations to be the catalyst for huge change for his members at The Business Wealth Club Scottsdale, Arizona as well as his one to one Coaching clients.

Doug actively employs superior communication, team building and Leadership skills, (Kolbe Certified) while he works with clients to resolve problems and he specializes in helping retail owners, CPAs and Attorneys.

His Coaching helps guide them in identifying their ideal customer, creating marketing plans, developing strategic planning and identifying strategies for accelerated business growth. Team building, leadership communication clarity and growing client loyalty are all Doug's strengths but that's just scratching the surface of what he can bring to the success of your business!

Doug is also the author of *What's In Your Head? The 7 Secrets to Retail Business Success*

THE 7 SECRETS TO ENTREPRENEURIAL ENLIGHTENMENT

THE ROADMAP TO ACHIEVING BUSINESS GROWTH

I first met Doug at the Partnership Seminar in the US in 2011 and we hit it off immediately, I think because we were there with the mind set of looking for opportunities to link up and build businesses. It was his track record of success and his commitment to his own personal development and knowledge growth that really impressed me.

Having worked closely with him to launch The Business Wealth Club opportunity into the US - his drive and passion is unstoppable, although he does keep telling me that he's in a hurry as he's getting old!

Not sure that's true as he has more energy than people I have met half his age :-)

I know that his track record in helping grow retail and e-commerce businesses makes him an expert in this area, but his ability to apply our Core Models and Frameworks to the Business Community he is building in Scottsdale is already delivering real results for his members.

If you can get to a club meeting of his I strongly suggest you do as you are in for a treat!

Keep up the good work Doug and I'm glad you're on our team...

— *Paul Avins*

SECRET #1: WHAT IS YOUR DEFINITION OF SUCCESS?

Lets start with a key question of what does success look like for you? Can you feel and describe it? So often as Entrepreneurs we buy into the Vision of Success based on what other people tell us, the media shows or seminar leaders sell us on!

Frequently many of my coaching clients when we first start working together, can't define success in their own terms and that can create energy blocks. Most describe it in terms of money and while that is an important and critical measurement, having a crystal-clear vision of what success looks like for you is fundamental to achieving profitability in your business.

I want you to focus on Why, What, and then How in that order...

Many businesses owners put their primary focus on the How or the What, but I have learned that by placing Why as the first consideration, it makes it easier for the other pieces to fall into place. (PA Post it - If you have a Big enough Why you'll figure out the How!)

If you have a Big enough Why you'll figure out the How!

Here's a reveling exercise - fill in the missing pieces in the following sentence. Once you do, you will begin to get very clear on what success might look like. Are you ready?

I love to help, serve and work with ....
Fill in the blank. Let's insert here who your ideal customer is or the target market that you want to go after.

For example, in my company, "I help retail business owners and manufacturers..."

Now let's fill in the next part of the sentence:

...do, or be, or get, or fix .... Fill in the blank and insert here the result that you can get for them or the problem you help them solve as people pay you to help them solve problems and get results.

Using my earlier example, "I help retail business owners and manufacturers attract more customers and sales..."

And now we'll insert into this sentence an adverb that defines your differentiator:......................................for example, are you faster, cheaper or make things easier for your customers, etc.)

My Coaching example reads like this: "I help retail business owners and manufacturers attract more "A" grade customers, Sales and Profits faster, easier and with less stress." Do you see how this sentence is beginning to define me and my business model Value?

Always important for a coach to walk his talk I'm sure you'll agree...

Now for the final part of the sentence...

...even if .... (and here I want you to insert the biggest objection you come up against).

So here is the complete sentence using my example: "I help retail business owners and manufacturers get more "A" grade customers, Sales and Profits faster, easier and with less stress even if they think it's impossible in their business, industry or location..."

The sentence that you write should give you a clear understanding of your value and your business, and can help to create a better picture of the success you want to achieve.

You create your life with every decision that you make and with every action or non-action you take. After all how you do one thing is often how you do everything!

Right now I want you to take a minute and do an exercise with me that I call "Imagine the Possibilities." When most people think about their business they do not think in terms of "How big or successful can I REALLY be?"

Imagining the possibilities, and then taking consistent positive action to get there, is a key step in obtaining business success. With that in mind, here are a couple of questions that I want you to answer...

SALES & MARKETING

- Can you see and feel your business as the leader in your market?

- Is your dream to be the "go-to person" or the "go-to business" in your market?

- What have you done to differentiate your business from your competitors?

Now that I have shared how to "Imagine the Possibilities," I also want you to practice something that I call "BIG Thinking" hay I'm an American and we are used to thinking on large scale because of the size of our market!

Now, I'm not talking about getting a bigger facility or a larger store / office or adding more and more locations just to impress other people. What I am talking about is learning to "think big" inside your own mind.

How BIG would you take your business if you knew you could not fail?

SECRET #2: CHOOSE ABUNDANCE

When you live and, more importantly, act in abundance, you will have highly motivated and loyal employees who become part of the success of your business. One of the keys to employee morale is treating them like you would like to be treated and when you treat Customers with abundance not only will the buy - they will refer as well and referrals are the best kind of leads because they already know about you and trust you. Every single customer should be considered special, how do I do that you may ask when you have so much to do every day? The answer is to treat them in abundance!!

Let's talk about coming from a position of lack for a moment. Lack is the opposite of abundance and is a negative mindset that can affect the whole business, and if not treated or stopped can even kill it's energy and profit potential. Is there an attitude of lack or abundance in your business? Do you have the mindset that all customers are just looking to get the cheapest price or that they are all trying to steal or cheat you in some way? How do you react when a Customer Complains or asks for a Refund? How do you embrace adversity? As an Opportunity to Grow or as a reason to contract and hide?

Make a commitment NOW to banish coming from a position of lack in your mind and business forever buy doing the exercise below:

White out 2 ways you can put more Abundance into your Business:

1. ....

2. ....

SECRET #3: YOUR SPECIAL ABILITY

This Secret is about doing what you love to do and doing it all day, every day. I'd like to begin by asking you to honestly answer the following questions:

- How do you spend your time while you are at work?

- Do you spend the majority of it "IN" your business and not "ON" your business?

- Are you running your business or is it running you?

- You spend your day doing a bunch of "stuff," but does any of this stuff get you more sales, more customers, or more profits?

When you focus on your special ability you maximize time, money, and effort. I firmly believe that the thing you do best is going to make you the most money in the shortest period of time by working on your strengths and letting others provide the support that you need to be successful.

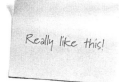
Really like this!

Let me share with you a story about a client who was getting bogged down in accounting paperwork and other administrative tasks that he hated every minute doing. When I asked my client what was it that he loved to do, he replied, "I love to sell and work with my customers." I suggested that if he spent his time selling and working with customers and hired a bookkeeper to do all the other tasks, he would be able to generate the additional sales needed to pay for the bookkeeper. He would then be a much happier owner. At first he resisted and argued about why it wouldn't work, funny how we often fight positive change, but finally agreed to give it a try. Now my client's business is thriving because of this very small shift in his mindset. He is working in his Special Ability, he has never been happier, and his business has never been more profitable!

Let me ask you that question again...

What is it that you love to do that will make you the most money, in the shortest time, with the least effort, and that will have the biggest on-going impact?

Do what you do best and don't stress about the rest!

SECRET #4: IT IS NOT ABOUT LUCK, HOW YOU DO ANYTHING

I often find with my clients that How they do anything is how they do everything!"

This is a small section because don't you think this statement speaks for itself? When you set the standard for excellence, and when you set the expectation for greatness, your customers and employees will react and follow your lead. It is very important for you to project a winning image as the leader in your business on a daily basis. You must see yourself as successful if you want others to see you in the same way.

What you have in your life is a direct reflection of what you believe and expect. What you put your focus on always multiplies - Positive or Negative as energy flows where attention goes.

In what ways do you need to shift your attention in your business right now?

SECRET #5: FAILURE

If you're not failing, then you are not pushing hard enough! Failure is just another word for Feedback and we all want more feedback in our business and lives don't we.

Risk taking is what entrepreneurial businesses are all about, so you need to start getting comfortable with being uncomfortable.

I've always thought that failure should be looked upon as a gift. Because when failure occurs it brings you that much closer to winning! Failure brings learning and learning leads to change and change leads to success. Have you ever considered the decisions you make when you operate from fear? I'll bet that they are not good ones. I know that this might sound a little crazy, but I want you to begin to welcome failure into your life - don't shy away from failure because of fear. After all, fear is only False Emotions Appearing Real!

A great Question to ask is "What's REALLY happening here?" Then write out the answers and read them back, you'll realise you have more power than you thought. Let your faith in your abilities become your parachute to see the possibilities in all the feedback you receive.

SECRET #6: PLANS AND THE 'LAW OF GOYA'

Now, we all know that successful plans should contain great strategy. It is a necessary key ingredient for their implementation. Let me share an outline with you for creating a step-by-step process for goal setting:

1. Become super clear on what your goals are.

2. Burn them into your subconscious mind.

3. Feed them continually: "these are my goals."

4. Imagine them in your mind.

5. Create a movie in your mind about your goals and keep playing it.

6. Then act as if you had already achieved the goals.

SALES & MARKETING

7. Always stay in gratitude for everything you have and want.

8. Celebrate when you begin to attract what you want in your life.

Let me take a minute now and tell you about a new law of business that I recently learned. It's called the "Law of GOYA."

Have you ever heard about it? GOYA stands for "Get Off Your Ass!" This means simply what is says, take a no-excuses approach to your business and get up and as they say at Nike, "Just do it!"

As Business Wealth Club Founder Paul Avins ofter says "You can make Money or Excuses - you just can't make both at the same time!"

Time to go to work....

SECRET #7: COMMUNICATION

I believe this last Secret it is the most powerful one there is for creating success in a retail business or any business.

The key to communicating in today's world is being authentic, being real, and being you. Your message must reflect your values, and your personality. People want to hear you!! I hope that you are telling both your employees and vendors what you want, and not making them guess.

Marketing and Advertising is also communicating. Focusing on a belief that you have to communicate price all the time is a HUGE mistake. People want to hear about your value, your solutions, and your benefits the Return on Investment (ROI) they'll receive when they buy from you.

Communicate your call to action very clearly - Ask for the SALE - it's your job!

Social media and the Internet (Web site) are fast and ever-changing emerging forms of communication. Yes there is a place for Facebook, Twitter, You Tube, and LinkedIn in your business, but develop a specific strategy and tactics and work the plan. Social media can be time consuming, confusing, and a waste of time and money if not planned carefully with a professional.

Remember this last and most powerful Secret, the Secret of Communication. Do it well and do it often for your business success! Practice the old adage of, "Tell them, tell them what you told them, and then tell them again!" Communications is the activator for all the pervious Secrets.

**NEW TECHNOLOGIES FOR
GENERATING LEADS, SALES AND
PROFITS HAVE EXPLODED IN THE
LAST FEW YEARS, OFFERING YOU
GLOBAL REACH FOR LITTLE OR
ZERO COST! LEARN HOW TO
MAXIMISE THIS POWERFUL
OPPORTUNITY...**

ONLIN
MARK

E
ETING

BILL
BELEW

Bill Belew, a.k.a. Wil.by is a professional blogger = he pays his sizeable Silicon Valley, USA mortgage through revenue generated purely from traffic at his network of blog sites. Bill has taken 10 different and unrelated blog topics to more than 1,000,000 unique visitors.

Bill writes about business in Asia, International News, Sports, the Environment, and being unashamed to be a Christian.

He claims his older son, a fine artist and award winning classical pianist got the right side of his brain, his younger son, a molecular exercise physiology scientist, got the left side of his brain and his princess daughter got all of his good looks because he has none left of all three. Bill did NOT dress the King.

FOUR ABSOLUTES TO
GET TRAFFIC
TO YOUR WEB SITE

I met Bill, The Traffic Professor at the Brendan Bruchard Partnership Seminar in the US. (Seminars like this are great places to Network). He's a very private person, a true family man, but also a man who is committed to making the world a better place by empowering business owners and individuals in countries the world over to drive traffic to their business or Blog without having to pay for it.

He has one of the most amazing track records I have ever come across and I am truly honoured that he has "broken cover" to share his never before put in print strategies with you. If you want more traffic to your site for FREE... read on.

— *Paul Avins*

> As of this writing, more than 35 million unique visitors searched out and found my websites. Those visitors flipped through more than 55 million pages in my network of sites. And ALL of them came because they were looking for me, for something I had that they wanted. I NEVER paid for traffic...NEVER. It is ALL FREE, organic, quality search engine traffic. I'll say again, these visitors came looking for me.

Not long ago I was in south San Francisco at an internet marketing conference with 300+ people many of whom had great ideas. A week or so after that I was in San Diego at another conference and a different group of 300+ people with more very good to great ideas. Back again in San Francisco (I live in the Bay Area just a few minutes' drive from Google, Yahoo!, Facebook and Apple) I attended AdTech 2011. There were hundreds of booths and thousands of attendees. The internet marketing folk, the AdTech folk ALL had something in common...they ALL wanted more traffic to their sites so they could peddle their ideas, services or wares. Everyone wants more traffic. **I know how to get more traffic.** Legitimate and relevant traffic.

The AdTech booths lured foot traffic with promises of free iPad2s and other goodies in exchange for email addresses. Attendees to each of the three events paid 1,000s of dollars just to be at these conferences in hope of partnering up with someone who could get them more exposure so that they MIGHT market their products better. That's okay but there's another way.

Did you know it is 62% cheaper to have someone come looking for you than it is for you to go looking for them? **Creating a well-trafficked blog** is much more cost efficient than shelling out money to set up a booth at a trade show. Applying good Search Engine Optimisation principles to your web site is much more effective and less costly than telemarketing. Exercising **good social media strategies,** of which a blog is still the best, makes much more sense while costing less cents than direct mail. A blog will allow you to say something longer than 140 characters, will attract people beyond your friends and acquaintances, and welcomes interactive communication/feedback. And, when appropriate you can still provide links from your blogs to your social circles via Twitter, Facebook, LinkedIn, Google+ and the like.

SOME QUICK FACTS:

- In the past 2 years US companies have doubled their budgets for blogs/social media

- Companies with blogs have 4.3 times more pages indexed than companies without = internet users find you NOT the other way around

- Companies with blogs get 2.4 times as many leads as companies without

- In 2010, nearly 7 in 10 internet users read blogs

- In 2011, more than 2 out of 5 companies had a blog

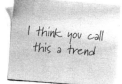

I think you call this a trend

Companies that update their sites regularly get 2.6 times more leads than those that don't.

The most pertinent questions are not "**Should** I blog? **Should** I have a blog at my site? Should I create a dynamic site to draw attention to my product?" but "**How can** I learn to blog better? **What does it take** to get good, quality, relevant traffic to my website?" If you're not blogging, you are far behind the curve. (For what it's worth, I use website, blog, blog site interchangeably. For the picky - a website is static, unchanging. A blog site is dynamic, updated regularly. A blog can refer to a site or an individual post within your site. To me, they are one and the same.)

There are **4 absolutes every blog must have in order to get traffic to their sites.**

1. A WEBSITE MUST HAVE A SUFFICIENT QUANTITY OF ARTICLES/POSTS TO GET NOTICED

I know people who say they have 20 articles or pages at their site. I know others who have 200 posts. I have more than 20,000. Call it the 'duh' factor. But it is absolutely fundamental –the more stuff you have at your website, the more findable you are. I have 1,000 times and 100 times, respectively, greater possibility of being found than the guy with 20 or 200 pages. Of course, if your goal is to reach a local market, you don't need 20,000 articles. You just need more pages/articles/posts than anyone else in your local niche who is competing for the same search engine ranking that you are. Simple as that. But it's not all about quantity. It's not just 'stuff.' You need quality.

Site	No. of posts	Traffic	Traffic/post
A	533	836,464	1,568.3
B	372	494,066	1,328.1
C	240	167,024	685.9

(Real results – Site A had 2.2 times the number of posts of site C, but more than 5 times the traffic.)

> **Lesson - Do more posts/updates than your competitor and you will get better results. Simple, eh?**

Simple yes – but very effective!

2. A WEBSITE MUST HAVE GOOD QUALITY ARTICLES

Good quality means the articles are written in such a way as to appeal to the search engines AND readers. I have heard from Google's top search engineers that there are some 220 variables that go into how they rank a page or a site. But there are only about 20 items if employed correctly, that will make up 90-95% of the difference in search engine results. The other 200 items will help improve a sites effectiveness by 5-10%. Problem is, people want to spend their time fiddling with the other 200 rather than working the 20 to get the most out of their effort.

Which is better. This? *"Look at me. My ten articles have perfect SEO. I just wish someone would read them."*

Or this? - *"Hundreds of people are asking me in the comments for more information about (insert your service here)."*

Here's one tip – For your title, imagine what words you would put into a search engine box to find the information you are plugging. Use those words in your title. Cute doesn't work. Spiffy doesn't work. Clever doesn't work. Seldom do people put an adjective or adverb in a search engine box. Clunky but reader–friendly works best. Use good titles and you are leaps and bounds ahead of the guy who is deciding where and when to use an H2 header, or which words should be bold case and which should not.

PanAsianBiz	
Entry Pages Ranked by Visits	
	Entry Page
478	http://www.panasianbiz.com/asi...xposes-undergraduate-students/
403	http://www.panasianbiz.com/edu...yderabad-jntu-ac-results-htno/
324	http://www.panasianbiz.com/asia/india/jntu-hyderabad-results/
169	http://www.panasianbiz.com/wor...ked-sara-jean-performing-yoga/
117	http://www.panasianbiz.com/ent...ran-johars-party-photos-video/
92	http://www.panasianbiz.com/mob...-review-features-photos-video/
86	http://www.panasianbiz.com/tec...eview-specifications-features/
73	http://www.panasianbiz.com/tac/jntu-ac-results-htno/
72	http://www.panasianbiz.com/asi...dianrail-irtc-railway-enquiry/
70	http://www.panasianbiz.com/edu...bareda-results-2011-announced/
69	http://www.panasianbiz.com/ent...es-specifications-photo-video/
65	http://www.panasianbiz.com/ind...p-of-china-the-15-most-useful/
43	http://www.panasianbiz.com/asi...st-know-facts-about-india-map/
41	http://www.panasianbiz.com/cat...cation/exam-results-education/
40	http://www.panasianbiz.com/asi...ds-2011-winners-photo-gallery/
34	http://www.panasianbiz.com/

(Good quality posts will rank in the SEs for a very long time!)

The circled posts were written years ago and still get searched out 100s of times daily.

> **Lesson – write good stuff. It is not as subjective as you think.**

3. A BLOG SITE MUST BE UPDATED REGULARLY.

Remember, *companies that update their sites regularly get 2.6 times more leads than those that don't*. Depending on your traffic goals and the size of the market you are appealing to, daily works. Multiple times daily works better. I know sites that update hourly and even several times an hour. They have a worldwide audience and their traffic reflects their effort and consistency. The answer for you is to update your site more often than your competitor does. Fundamentally, the more often a website is updated, the more often the searchbots come to see what is going on. The more often the bots come the more they think (if bots could think) something new is here, resulting in a step up in search engine ranking appeal. Makes sense?

> **Lesson – update your site more often than your competitor.**

4. STAY WITH IT LONG ENOUGH TO CATCH ON

The number one reason why businesses fail is that the business doesn't or can't stay around till the idea catches on. Not enough seed money. Supplier goes missing. Divorce. Relocation. Whatever. Something comes up to keep the business from continuing. If the business is a good idea to begin with it's most often a good idea to dog until it catches on...no matter what. A blog is no different.

Think in terms of months to get the best results. To be sure, ranking, exposure and traffic can be achieved in a short time. But it can and usually does disappear just as quickly. The longer it takes to build something up, the longer it takes for it to disappear.

Another great principle – the harder you try, the harder it is to give up. If you put enough blood, sweat and tears into building your online presence, you will not be able to abandon it too easily. If you are prone to give up on your site, it's because you haven't tried hard enough yet. It's that simple. (There is a point when a site will catch on and the traffic takes off). Not a few people will work hard for 3, 4, 5 or 6 months and conclude, "Bill lied to me." Then quit. This site took off in the 10th month.

> **Lesson – if you're giving up, first ask yourself how long have you been at it?**

THE BIG QUESTIONS

Of course, everyone wants to know regarding QUANTITY – how many is a lot? Regarding QUALITY – what are those 20 must–knows? Regarding CONSISTENCY – how often is often? And regarding LONGEVITY - how long does it take to catch on?

These are questions that TheTrafficProfessor will answer. In TheTrafficProfessor, I tell you **how many posts, how many words, how many days** overall and at *what pace* I wrote to see the first 1,000,000 visitors to my sites. Use my metrics as a sign post or measuring stick and apply yourself accordingly. A person who gets 1,000,000 visitors can always get 100,000. The reverse of that is not true.

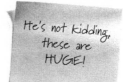

He's not kidding, these are HUGE!

I really do want you to achieve your traffic goals. If your idea is good, why shouldn't people know about it? If it's really good you might even have a moral obligation to get the word out.

NEXT STEPS

There are 34,000 searches done every second! More than 2,000,000 searches each minute. And as many as 3 billion searches done EACH day. Why shouldn't people be finding you? It's not hard. It's not easy. Blogging is a way to be found and I can teach you how.

www.thetrafficprofessor.com/buynow

www.billbelew.com

ONLINE MARKETING

RON
DAVIES

Declared the "Obvious Choice" by New York Times Best-Selling Business author Elsom Eldridge, Ron works with business owners in Canada, the US, and the UK helping them better leverage social media and the Internet for real ROI. His unique strategies have a profound impact on corporate bottom line through laser-focused social media, brand building and monitoring automation & mobile device leverage.

A decorated war veteran with 23 years of service to his country, Ron started the first of his two companies in 1998. Ron is the CEO of Blue Monster Marketing, an interactive offline marketing company located in Trenton, Ontario, providing coaching & consulting to businesses & professionals who want the Internet to work hard for them. Ron exploded onto the public speaking scene quickly becoming one of the most in-demand speakers in his field.

One of Ron's clients proclaimed, "Ron literally turned my business website around in a single 15 minute conversation, and all he did was glance at it!" Dennis Becker, speaking event organizer, said of Ron's presentation, "Ron absolutely wowed attendees with his presence, passionate delivery and skills".

LEVERAGING THE BLUE MONSTER
FACEBOOK
FOR OFFLINE BUSINESS

In the world of Online Marketing, Facebook Ads and Affiliate Marketing, there is more hype than substance. This is exactly why, when I wanted coaching in this area I sought out a man with not only a personal track record of success, but also with real world RESULTS for clients that I wanted to emulate.

Ron was the man I identified with and even though he was over the pond in Canada (Skype Coaching works great!) I found his knowledge, insights and blend of online and offline business experience extremely valuable.

He is a man who proves you really can build a huge business largely on auto pilot and live the lifestyle you want while enjoying the ultimate Entrepreneurial prize - Freedom.

I'm grateful that he took time out of his summer holiday in the mountains to contribute this power-packed chapter...

— *Paul Avins*

> For local business owners, Facebook is the ultimate secret weapon. It's really all about "Likeability".

The biggest problem brick-and-mortar business owners face when it comes to the Internet has been converting that virtual community into foot traffic through the doors of their shops or getting phones to ring at their sales desks, be it repeat customers, or new business. The expenditure of money and time in the online realm has with only rare exception actually translated into any kind of measurable ROI, with businesses forced to deal with website companies, PPC experts, and so forth. The sad reality is that very few website or Internet presence companies know anything at all about direct marketing, but do know just enough to dazzle and befuddle offline business people, and as such, the trusting business owner is often their easy prey.

> Enter Facebook, the perfect nesting ground for any business, online or offline for far too many reasons for us to cover here, but just to get started, how about the fact that your company will be positioned in the center of over 750,000,000 users?

Doesn't it make sense that it is much easier to sell to people that you are surrounded by, than to attract them to you from miles away? That's precisely why Facebook is so powerful. We speak to people about what they are interested in, while standing in the community where the average user spends an astonishing 3 hours every day!

"But Ron" you shout, "We already have people doing Google for us!". Tsk tsk! Google is already in the shadow of Facebook in terms of the number of LOCAL business searches, and the truth is that those highly-touted "Google Places" listings are getting hacked every day, with black-hat marketers potentially editing the phone number and link of YOUR business to the one owned by the competitor that hired them. It happens every day.

Did you know you can add your business to Facebook local search right now, without a mouse, without a computer, just a smart phone, and all you need do is stand in your shop, open the free Facebook application, and use the "Check In" function. This will create a geo-located listing of your business, and you will show up instantly for every Facebook user in the area, plus you will be indexed by Google. All for $0. Do I have your attention?

When people are at home, or at work, they leave Facebook running in the background. It is where they hang out, talk to family, network, research purchases, you name it.

> **I believe that as a direct result of social media giants, in this case Facebook, that the information age is over, and the referral age has begun.**

You will see me Swipe and Deploy this line!

I say this because the viral component of sharing of Facebook is far, far more powerful a marketing tool than any piece of ad copy on any flyer. Imagine being able to target a buyer right down to age, sex, what they discuss on Facebook, the postal code they are in, or even send them a coupon exactly on their birthday... How powerful is that? Not to mention that the integrated Facebook advertising system allows you to get clicks for as little as two or three cents, the same clicks that Google charges fifty cents for, and of course Google has little chance of accomplishing the kind of targeting that Facebook ads can.

Then there is the free advertising: Simple add "Like us on Facebook to join our VIP Club!" to the top of your cash register receipt printer, and a static cling sticker to your window with similar text.

ONLINE MARKETING

> **Just by bringing existing customers back in this way, you will add an easy 20% to your sales. In addition, you can now announce events, and offer coupons that will be shared virally with all of their friends. Free. Viral. Marketing. Getting the picture?**

Now, if you already have a website, you can even integrate Facebook's incredible "Social Plugins" that will allow others to market for you. It essentially puts Facebook's viral capability right into your existing site or blog! This means people can "Like" your existing site, which is shared virally. Cool!

Another important part of Facebook marketing are the "Groups" and "Events". If you own a surfer shop, for example, you can search the term "Surfing" on Facebook and you will find dozens of groups with literally hundreds of thousands of members. By joining the group, and posting your "Event" (Could be a sale on surf boards, for example), all of those group members will be notified by Facebook, and all will receive an email directly from Facebook on your behalf. Free marketing, laser-targeted, and very invited by users.

An interesting extension of this is the fact that many users do their "Facebooking" via smart phone, and will receive text or SMS messages about your event instantly.

Now, there are three very, very important things to remember when getting set up on Facebook:

1 When you initially join Facebook, you have what is called a "profile". This is NOT a Facebook page. It is your personal profile. Now, under that profile, you have the ability to create countless Facebook "Pages". These pages are for your business. When you create a "Page", Facebook gives you a whole treasure-trove of tools, including the ability to do what is called a "Fan gate". A Fan gate is simply a dynamic event that allows you to change what people see on your Facebook page after they click the "Like" button. Remember, Facebook is all about the "Like". That is what makes it viral, and opens the line of communication between you and your visitor/customer.

ALWAYS incentivise the "Like". For example "Like us now and receive 20% of your first order", or "Like us now and receive a free pack of golf tees". Once they have "Liked" your page, every time you post to it, they will be notified, plus the "Like" itself shows up on THEIR profile, and is seen by everyone that has friended them.

The "Like" can be likened (ahem :) to a mailing list, without the risk of spam. It also tells all of that person's friends that they "Liked" your page, inviting them to do the same. This "Fan gate" capability can even simply result in a video from YouTube that explains to the person how to collect the incentive you are offering. We recommend to our clients that they use QR codes that allow the Facebook user to simply scan the code and redeem the coupon automatically.

Get my special offers by scanning our QR Code (Quick Response Code) at the back of this book!

2 The second important point is the creation of what is called an "Alias" or "Username" on Facebook for your page. A username looks like http://fb.com/USERNAME . This could be the name of your store, or better yet, a search term people might use to look for the product or service you offer. An example would be http://fb.com/pizzadelivery. By the way, http://fb.com part is simply a shortened version of http://facebook.com, and works exactly the same for usernames.

In order to get a username, you simple need to drum up 25 "Likes" to your page, which you can do very easily by sharing your new page with your existing Facebook friends, or by using a very cool site called Fiverr.com to hire someone to get you those critical 25 likes for a mere $5. Good deal!

ONLINE MARKETING

3 Facebook gives you some very powerful tools to monitor not only the success of your advertising on Facebook, but also information on the demographics of the people visiting and "Liking" your page. This allows very accurate targeting. This is done through a system called "Facebook Insights". Insights will tell you everything you could ever want to know about not only the visitors and "Likers" of your Facebook page, but also about those that visited your own website or blog, so long as you have implemented the "Social Plugins" mentioned earlier in this chapter.

A little more on "Social Plugins". This under-used feature of your Facebook account allows you to provide an open, though moderated, place for visitors to your website to share your business with others, leave comments, ask for help, etc. Essentially, this gives you an opportunity to be a "benevolent expert", helping your customers and visitors, building trust, and attracting them to use your business. People like to deal with businesses they know, businesses that are approachable, accountable, and transparent, and a presence on Facebook affords you all of these things.

> **Don't make the mistake of thinking that a Facebook presence is time consuming. It really isn't. I have a client that is a restaurant, and each day the chef creates a video with his smart phone of him reviewing the day's menu. He simply posts the video to Facebook. This is all built in to the Facebook smart phone app.**

In fact, one of the motorcycle dealership chains that we consult for publishes all of their events live onto Facebook using a free smart phone application called "Ustream". They have a trailer load of motocross bikes and ATV's at racing events, and stream live action to their page. Imagine how this could be used for your business...

The possibilities are limitless, constrained only by your imagination. This is about opening the communication between you and your existing customers, as well as being very inviting and incentivising to gain new customers. They are in your town using Facebook right now. Help them find you, know you, like you, and trust you. That is when they will buy from you, and continue to buy from you.

It's all about "Likeability".

NEXT STEPS

Find out more about Ron and how he transforms the businesses he works with at:

www.BlueMonsterMarketing.com

Have a look at this Web Site for an Out Of The Box approach – I love it!

ONLINE MARKETING

GARY FOX

Along with his team at Tribal Cafe, a digital marketing agency, Gary Fox is focused on helping businesses stay competitive in an increasingly tough and competitive world by using social media, web and mobile platforms to create new and exciting ways to drive growth.

Gary has previously worked for large and small companies in sales and marketing both in the UK and across Europe.

He has worked on large scale integrated marketing campaigns for brands such as Nike, HP, Microsoft, Gillette and Nokia. In addition to holding an MBA in digital marketing from Warwick Business School, Gary's skills have been honed by harnessing technology in marketing to provide unique and innovative solutions for clients.

WHY BRANDS USE
FACEBOOK

My wife Sue is addicted to FaceBook, and it has bugged me for some time that although she uses it socially – as a business we weren't harnessing it's powers for our benefit. I'm a great believer in the Law of Attraction - so it was no surprise to me that once I set my intention to find a resource for this information, shortly afterwards Gary appeared!

He had come along to a Social Media Workshop that Business Wealth Club Mentor Dave Griffin was running for one of my Corporate Clients – and Dave thought we should talk. I am glad we did and when you read his chapter, you'll understand why. So, if like me you want to make Facebook part of your Online Marketing strategy going forward – get a pen and paper out before starting to read Gary's tip-filled chapter!

— *Paul Avins*

> Facebook has grown since its origins in 2004 to be the largest global social network with over 750m people using it (that is 1 in every 3 people on the internet). During this time it has moved from being used principally by college kids to now having an average user age of 35.

Brands like Coca Cola, Nike, Disney, Sony, Samsung and many others are spending large amounts of money on promoting their Facebook brand page and using Facebook to engage with their customers. These brands use Facebook pages to develop a community around their brand. In 2010 Pepsi, for the first time in 23 years, did not have commercials on the Super Bowl. Instead, they spent $20 million on a social media campaign called, The Pepsi Refresh Project, where users give ideas to Pepsi for ways to refresh their communities.

If it's good enough for Pepsi...!

In fact, you're likely to spot the shift as brands advertise their Facebook pages on television commercials. But it is not just big brands that can use Facebook as part of their marketing strategy. Businesses of all sizes can harness the power of Facebook to market their business using the platforms built-in tool kit.

HOW CAN YOUR BUSINESS USE FACEBOOK

Before you make your plan for how you are going to market your business on Facebook you need to understand its capabilities. What you ultimately decide to do with your Facebook needs to fit to your overall marketing strategy and objectives. This includes the customisation of your Facebook page, the content you post and how you interact with your Facebook community.

The focus of your community will be your Facebook page and much like a website, a page can be branded and have similar functionality e.g. email capture forms, video embedded, links...but the real power comes in the ability for people to like and share your content. This generates valuable word of mouth marketing bringing more potential customers to your Facebook page and extends the reach of your business.

TIPS TO IMPROVE YOUR FACEBOOK PAGE

Investing in a good website design, layout and search engine optimisation pays back in the long run. Likewise how much you invest both in terms of planning and customisation for your Facebook page will affect the number of followers you gain and how your conversion rates. Here are some simple ideas on how you can customise your business page:

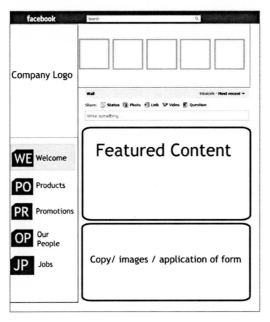

Example framework of a page with customised tabs

Capture leads directly from your Facebook page (email/contact details...)

Feature your products or services. Have a tab detailing your products or services (use a video)

ONLINE MARKETING

Promote your products or services. Set a tab for promotions and regularly rotate this with different specials for your Facebook followers (make the promotion exclusive to Facebook)

Your People. People buy from people so create a space and talk about your people, if you are a small company this is ideal to put over some personality about your business.

Recruitment. Use this to effectively advertise job positions, ask for people to share and spread the news. Some businesses have dramatically reduced the cost of hiring people this way.

HOW TO USE THE FACEBOOK TOOL KIT

The Facebook tool kit for businesses comprises of the following:

Advertising – a powerful and highly target ad. platform. Facebook advertising allows you to target people based on location, age, gender, birthday, sexual preference, relationship status, language, interests, education status, educational institution and work place.

Event marketing – a built in functionality to actively promote events to your community and beyond through sharing. Combine this with the advertising platform and you can target a much broader audience.

Deals – a promotional platform particularly targeted at leisure, retail and restaurant businesses.

Facebook stores – Businesses can sell their products directly within Facebook and many retailers and businesses are seizing this opportunity e.g. Asos. Each time someone buys a product it is featured in their newsfeed and creates trusted endorsement of your product as well as word of mouth marketing.

8 QUESTIONS TO ASK BEFORE YOU START

None of us has the time or resources to do anything that is not helping us achieve our mission as an organization or company. Some of the main questions you need to ask are focused on what you are trying to achieve as a business and how they relate to meeting your customer's needs.

1. Who are your customers?

2. Do you understand why they buy your products or services?

3. Are your customers, clients and the people you want to connect with using Facebook?

4. Are your competitors active in this space?

5. What influences your customers?

6. What do they value?

7. What problems can you help them solve?

8. What value can you add through using Facebook?

Grab your pen and write these down!

SET YOUR OBJECTIVES

Lay out a plan that will help achieve the company's objectives and achieve tangible results. Here are a few ways that businesses can use Facebook:

- Traffic to your website – unique visits

- Engagement with your brand – traffic/views/comments, likes

- Word of Mouth – number of shares, mentions, links, likes

- Email/Newsletter – number of subscribers captured on Facebook

- Sales of products through Facebook store

10 STEPS TO FACEBOOK MARKETING

Here are ten trusted and proven steps in making sure you develop an effective Facebook marketing plan:

1. Plan and research. Take time to research how your competitors are using Facebook, look at case studies on Slide Share, listen to what customers are saying and doing on Facebook and produce a plan.

2. Your Facebook page. Your brand is valuable so it is important to invest in making it look good on Facebook. It will help you stand out from your competition. When you customise your Facebook page focus on how you want customers to interact with you.

3. Promote Your Page. Use Facebook advertising to target and build your community. Reward your Facebook community with exclusive promotions, competitions, polls, video content...

4. Integrate Your Facebook Page. Make sure you include your Facebook url in your email footer, any printed materials and on any posters and fully integrate it into your other marketing processes.

5. Recognise Your Followers. Make note of those people that contribute/comment and are active on your page and reward them with recognition and occasionally a surprise gift/reward.

6. Post Regularly. Fans need to feel that there is a reason for them to check into your Facebook page, but content posted too frequently will be considered spam; it is also the 2nd most cited reason for unfriending a fan page. The best choice is generally thought to be 2-3 posts a day.

7. Make It Conversational. Don't just post up information about your business. Use informative articles that help your customers as well. Ask questions but keep them simple to answer. It is important to embed ideas, spark conversation, and inspire others to take part and contribute content and thoughts.

8. Test Out Calls To Action. Ultimately you want people to take notice of your promotions, products or services. You need to have a defined process for how you want to convert customers; don't leave it to chance. Develop a clear call to action and experiment with which ones are most effective.

9. Be responsive. Have a clear policy on your page that tells people what your policy is for Facebook. If you have fair complaints posted on Facebook deal with them promptly, acknowledge people and be responsive. Simply deleting these posts can cause others to be suspicious of your business.

10. Use Your Followers to Grow. People often become very attached to active communities and passionate about the business, particularly if there is a personal connection to it. Ask your followers to recruit other people, provide incentives to do this. Also post up and highlight active followers – make them feel special and they in turn will reward you with loyalty and more followers.

NEXT STEPS

If you want to find out how you can further develop your business on Facebook then contact TribalCafe at:

www.tribalcafe.co.uk

if you quote TC97S7 in an email to: gary@tribalcafe.co.uk

we will send you a free eBook on how to grow your business on Facebook.

www.facebook.com/thetribalcafe

DAVE GRIFFIN

Dave has over 30 years experience of working within some of the toughest and most demanding organizations in the world. He is also a successful Entrepreneur in his own right running several businesses of his own and building a £2.4 million property empire in just 10 months using none of his own money! He's been responsible for P&L's worth over £2 million as well as delivering strong growth in difficult and demanding markets.

In 2005 he was struck down and became bedridden with ME for 8 months. He spent two years in a wheelchair but he never let this "excuse" stop him moving forward.

Having been a member of the Business Wealth Club in Oxford Dave decided to step up and work with the Founder Paul Avins to open two Franchise Clubs of his own in Newbury and Winchester.

"My goal is to create a positive and supportive environment for local business owners to learn how to be more effective in accelerating their sales, profits and success using tried, tested and proven techniques. Together we'll create a unique atmosphere where we all help each other be more truly successful than we could ever imagine being on our own."

SUPERCHARGE YOUR
SOCIAL MEDIA

Dave and I first met at a Marcus de Maria Wealth Workout Seminar where I was one of the guest speakers.

We stayed in touch and several years later he joined my Oxford Business Wealth Club even though it was a 1.5 hr drive for a 7 am start! Just 6 short months later he was stepping up to run our first franchised Club in Newbury which has been a storming success in it's first year, accelerating the sales, profits and success of his members and their businesses.

During the time we have worked together Dave has worked hard on himself to Master Social Media and has become one of the top UK experts in this dynamic area with 7,569 connections on Linked In, 13,500 Twitter followers & 3,429 Facebook friends.

He's also run a Social Media Roadshow across the UK for my Motor Industry Clients. I am proud and honored to have him on the team and to call him a friend... even though he has more followers than me!

– Paul Avins

ONLINE MARKETING

> **Welcome to a new era... social media marketing is being touted as the strategy that all businesses should be using... but should you? Is it right for your business and will it deliver you REAL results?**

We are in a new world, post the financial collapse. Rather than the days of old where people had products and actively sought their target market and made a pitch, now it is all about engagement and connecting to your customers in new environments, building trust and then adding value, the sales follow the value.

In fact you may not even be in front of your customers in a sales capacity at all, but rather conversing on facebook, twitter or another social media platform where somebody has recommended you as a person for a product your company has.

> **The original concept of *Return on Investment* completely goes out of the window and is replaced by *Return on Interaction*.**

Love this change in meaning!

Yes you can still test and measure returns... but now the focus is on engagement, interaction and conversations rather than conversion figures.

Recent figures are suggesting that 90% of us buy on recommendation... even from people we have never actually met. Studies on social media show that the average conversion rate on a website shoots from 7% buying to 71% when recommended via social networks. Now for me that is a figure I would like to explore more. It is more likely that when people ask for help or search for something they want, those they are connected to will pitch in so that when they arrive at your website they are already far more focused than someone arriving via a random search.

Understand this and you can take traffic from your competition who may out rank you right now in SEO terms on Google.

To succeed in Business and Social Media it takes planning, action and focus … you'll be in the right place at the right time more of the time. Randomly tweeting to the world will not achieve this, contrary to what most people believe.

KEY QUESTIONS TO ASK YOURSELF TO STAY ON TRACK:

- Decide WHO you want to connect to

- WHY you may be able to help each other

- Find out Where they are and What they need

- See What synergy may exist to create a win win

- Who you already know Who would be useful to them as a connection

… do you see a pattern forming here? Then welcome to the new world of sharing and helping others that is the essence of how social media works. It is the wine bar or village on-line where you know everyone's name and what they do, who to call on when you have a leaking tap or need a dressmaker, and you recommend people automatically because they are already in your mind.

Social media is not about expecting a reward for recommending a business or service, that is not to say it doesn't happen, of course it does and there are some great joint ventures out there doing exactly that. It is about giving before you receive and your reward will often not come from the source you gave to. It may be that they mention you to someone they know who in turn passed on your comments or helpful advice to someone who needs what you do. By delivering practical expert advice, being available and accessible - you set yourself up for success.

If you are in business, you want and need visibility and as social media is just about the best way of raising your profile quickly, it is also a great medium for generating your own Public Relations news.

Whether you like it or not your business is all over the internet. Get used to it as it is only set to accelerate in that respect. Perhaps it's one of the thousand of directories that feed from places like yell.com and have added your company to their list. Or maybe one of the many industry specific consumer review web sites like Tripadvisor.com - where customers can say just how good or bad they have found dealing with you: denying these have a direct result on your sales and profits and is a recipe for business disaster.

If you are not listening, you are missing out. Especially if the feedback is negative. There are some very simple social media tools on the market for monitoring just what is being said about your brand or service or in fact your competition!

These Include:

Put time in your diary now to set these up.

search.twitter.com – allowing you to search through Tweets by key words

Greplin is a search bar that aims to find desired results as it navigates through your social world.

Google Social Search helps you discover relevant content from your social connections

Some other social search engines like **socialmention.com** can be used along with **Google Alerts** to track what's being said about your business 24/7, now that's a smart use of technology.

These tools are free and will email you when something is said about your business or brand so you can interact. If it is negative, get involved and see if you can turn it around and sort it out, good customer service pays dividends online as offline!

If the feedback is positive, this is great news and interacting is usually a great way of making your customer feel even better and appreciated. Often just a simple thank you is all that is necessary and shows the wider market you are a proactive company to deal with.

> **Remember if you are not listening to your customers online… some of your competition probably are!**

In May 2010 Facebook overtook Google as the first place that people search for goods and services so your business needs to have a presence there.

It is inexpensive and you can even have a website presence, and lots of special offers that they can share with their on-line and real friends getting your company even more exposure. Social media is certainly not a fad, just like mobile phones were not a fad… but it does take some careful consideration of what it can do for your business and how much time you should be dedicating to it.

Without this you run the risk of joining the ranks of those who say it doesn't work because they idled away their time on-line broadcasting to people who were never listening!

Here are my top 5 Steps to getting started with *Social Media Success*:

 # FACEBOOK

Use this platform as the hub of all your marketing activities both online and offline. Drive traffic to a welcome tab on your Facebook Business page where prospective customers can interact with you and create a community. Do not make the mistake that a lot of businesses do by driving traffic to a non-interactive website.

ONLINE MARKETING

LINKEDIN

Use the powerful advanced search facilities within Linkedin to find and connect with your target market. Once connected you can then start building your relationship with your new contacts. A great way to bypass the gatekeepers and connect directly with decision makers.

YOU TUBE

You now can have your very own free TV channel so make the most of this by uploading tips videos, client testimonials etc. As Google owns You Tube it gives a heavy weight rating to videos in search results which means it is easier to get your video onto page 1 of Google than through SEO.

TWITTER

Build a following and immediately start using Twitter Search to listen for your name, your competitor's names, words that relate to your space. (Listening always comes first.) Then start discussions with people about their interests to start building the relationship. Share links to interesting articles, videos or blogs. Do not try and sell early on as this will just turn people off.

BLOGGING

Start a business blog and aim to blog at least twice weekly. The giant edge that blogging has over other types of online communication is that the content is always fresh. Nothing is ever allowed to stagnate. Blogging is not only about the written word either. It can encompass videos, photos, etc. In fact if writing doesn't come easy to you then a video blog (Vlog) may be the way to go. Blogging has a tremendously wide appeal to numerous people and they love to share what they read with other people. The more they like it, the more they'll share it.

I look forward to meeting up with you online!

NEXT STEPS

Connect with me online:

www.linkedin.com/in/davidapgriffin

www.facebook.com/TheBerkshireBusinessConsultant

www.twitter.com/bizcopilot

www.Newbury-BusinessWealthClub.co.uk

ONLINE MARKETING

125

ANDREW ROBERTS

A business owner for 10 years, Andrew built one of the largest business coaching companies in Australia with sales greater than $2m per annum. Passionate about entrepreneurship, Andrew has also started and run 4 further companies.

Inspired by the 4 hour workweek by Tim Ferris, Andrew sold his coaching company, in pursuit of building a business that remains small, but makes great money with lots of leverage.

Unsure where to start, he was on Facebook one night and registered for his first Webinar, which was being run out of London 1 week later and had people from more than 30 countries listening in. Inspired, he invested £1500 into the course that was on offer. To his amazement the girl running the Webinar made over £60,000 from that one hour selling an online course. Andrew had found his calling. He set up and ran his first Webinar and generated $9000!

He then went on to master Webinars a few years ago and its now his main strategy for generating leads and sales for his business. Because of the results he was achieving, he decided to create an arm to his business helping others learn and master this skill. www.howtowebinar.com

CREATE MORE SALES
IN A ONE HOUR
WEBINAR
THAN MANY CAN MAKE IN AN ENTIRE MONTH

Andrew and I met when we were both top Coaches in the World's No1 Business Coaching Franchise - Action Coach. One of the best things about the Franchise Network was connecting with other inspiring Coaches and Mentors such as Andrew at Global Conferences all around the World. He is based in Sydney, Australia not somewhere I go networking very often! Recently we both met up while attending The Info Marketing Summit in the US and I was amazed by the results he has been generating with his clients using Webinars.

I wanted Andrews view point in this book because it appears that it is getting harder and harder to get people to come to events or exhibitions in todays market as peoples time becomes more and more valuable. I'm certainly helping my coaching clients make a big part of their marketing plan revolve around Webinars... and Andrew will continue to be my Coach in this key business accelerating strategy and you're about to learn why...

— *Paul Avins*

> The webinar (or online seminar) is an extraordinary modern way to get your message, product or service in front of thousands of people. It's cheap to set up (many software providers allow you to run them for free), you can run them from anywhere in the world (you just need to have a good internet connection) and thousands of people can tune in live to watch you present and educate them about why they need your product or service.

HOW CAN WEBINARS FIT IN YOUR BUSINESS?

Burn out is the number one reason many entrepreneurs have to close their doors.

This is the way that most entrepreneurs run their business:

Generate 1 lead > Quality lead > 1 appointment > Maybe make sale > Follow up

You see most business owners will generate a lead, maybe qualify the lead, have a meeting, go out and maybe make a sale, and if they don't, then keep following up until the prospect either buys or stops returning your calls.

Compare this to running a Webinar. You put some advertising around the Webinar (I'm going to talk about some strategies shortly). The Marketing allows many to register for your Webinar. You spend an hour with them, you invite them to purchase. When you get good at it you can make multiple sales at once.

Launch Webinar > Run Webinar to many
> Make 1 to many sales > Record webinar
> Post Webinar for followup sales
> Auto the process to make passive sales

And when you get great at this you can automate the entire process so you don't even have to be there to run your presentation.

Have a look at
www.howtowebinar.com/onlinetraining

What is exciting about this is it leads to money so much faster. Many, many people get to hear your sales message and you're acting with speed.

Leverage speed! Fantastic!

Here is a great example

Ben is a personal friend of mine

He started his business only a couple of years ago and like most "sensible" new business owners, he planned to start slowly, one client at a time. I influenced Ben to try Webinars. Like many people, Ben kept saying 'I'm not ready for this and I don't believe I am very good presenter"

I told Ben, "If you can talk to your computer, then you're going to be fine."

Ben ran a couple of Webinars and didn't get much of a result. I then gave Ben some simple consulting and gave him access to our Webinar fast start program (you can have a look at this at www.howtowebinar.com/faststart)

Here is a summary of Bens results:-

- 85 people paid $85 each to listen to Ben's presentation

- Ben offered a course at the back end of his Webinar and generated an additional $9000

- Ben also signed up 6 clients onto his 1 to 1 Coaching Program – a further $6k per month of revenue coming into his business

- Total Return to Ben for the 1 hour Webinar - $34180

ONLINE MARKETING

On top of this, once you deliver a great Webinar, you record it and then automate it.

> *> Run a great Webinar > Record it*
> *> Automate your marketing system to point to the recording*
> *> Systemise the conversion process*
> *> Have someone else look after all low value tasks*
> *> Generate results passively and move onto next project*

This frees up so much time for you and helps you avoid burnout

HOW TO GET PEOPLE LINED UP AND EXCITED ABOUT YOUR SESSIONS

It's very important that you get people showing up for your Webinar.

McDonalds do not make the best hamburgers in town, yet they know how to market and sell the most.

Likewise, you don't have to have the greatest presentation or topic in town. You need to know how to market it well.

The number one thing that constitutes a successful Webinar is the topic.

In order to get big numbers on a Webinar you either:

- Choose a topic that people are searching for or

- Select a niche market

Your title is king. Compare these examples:

"How to grow your consulting business" versus

"A five step blueprint to add seven to ten new high paying clients to your consulting business in the next 60 days without cold calling".

In addition to a great title, you also need a registration page. The Webinar platform that we use allows you to set up a registration page. Here is an example:

How 10 Australian personal trainers went from training one to one to millionaires in less than 5 years

Webinar Registration

In this free 60 minute information packed webinar, we are interviewing one of Australias authrities when it comes to working with personal trainers and getting them results.

Mark Capelin is regarded as one of the greatest business minds in the personal training industry. Mark has worked with 10 of the largest personal training studios in Australia. One of his clients, currently operates the largest personal training studio in the world (they do close to 800 sessions per week).

All of the people Mark has worked with, were once personal trainers who are now millionaires because they learnt how to create success within this industry.

PT Train has lined up a once off intereview to hear Mark share his knowledge as to how these personal trainers get their results, and how if you followed this advice, you can get the same results.

In the jam peacked 1 hour webinar, Mark is going to teach you:-

1. The top strategies right now for growing your PT business (there are some secrets he will reveal that you just dont want to miss)

2. How over 10 of his clients went from being a one to one personal trainer to now operating multi million dollar personal training studios

There is a strong title, a paragraph introducing the Webinar and some bullet points about what people will take away from your 1 hour presentation.

The fastest way to start to get registrations is to your current contacts. My advice is going around and pooling all your contacts, all business cards, everyone you've ever met, and coming up with a topic that will add value to them. If you find that you don't have that list or you don't have that database at all, the fastest way possible is the joint venture or partnership. You approach someone else who's targeting your niche and you ask them to promote your Webinar.

If you approach someone else who has a list of your target audience (that you don't compete directly with) and ask them to market your Webinar to their list, you instantly pull people from their list onto yours. This is one of the main strategies we use.

(By the way – if you have a list of entrepreneurs that would like to learn about Webinars, please contact us so we can run a webinar to your list. Email us at support@howtowebinar.com)

Once people have registered, you also want a system to ensure they show up. Make sure you send a few emails to keep them in the loop. These should also encourage them to be excited about learning your information.

There are many other ways you can get people to register for your Webinars: Social Media, Guest Blogging, Google Advertising,

ONLINE MARKETING

fax Outs and Direct Mail are just a few examples. Watch our complimentary training at www.howtowebinar.com to learn more.

Sam Bowden is a vet who also runs a business called 'The United Vets Group'. (unitedvetsgroup.com) United Vets Group is a buyers group for vets.

His marketing wasn't getting him the results that he was after, until he came and did our Webinar programme.

Here are his results from Sam's third Webinar:

- Direct mail and fax campaign to 500 vets
- 65 people registered and 45 showed up
- 15 sales @$397 per month
- Life time value of a client is 3 years
- Total return for Sam on that 1 hour webinar $214,380 (25% increase in his business)

The big point that I want to make here, is you don't even need that many people on your Webinar to get the big results.

IT'S WHAT YOU PRESENT AND HOW YOU PRESENT IT THAT COUNTS

The key to getting people registered and showing up for your Webinar is running something of value – usually something that will fix a problem that your target audience is struggling with.

Here is the Webinar success formula that will help you achieve amazing results.

- Strong introduction. What can you say to get people really excited and leaning in at the start of your Webinar – glued to your screen?
- Stick strategy. What can you do to stick people to the end (so they don't decide half way through they have had enough)

- Sales Story. You really need to use a sales story that connects with your audience

- 2 – 3 pieces of core content. Less is often more. Don't present too much information

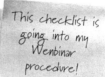

This checklist is going into my Wenbinar procedure!

- Transition to close. You need to master the *art of teaching* and the *art of next steps*

NEXT STEPS

There is a real art to learning this formula, and I highly recommended that you watch our online training at:

www.howtowebinar.com/onlinetraining

When you get good at this, I believe your conversion rates can be higher with a Webinar presentation than through one-to-one sales.

To learn more, visit www.howtowebinar.com to download a free ebook and register for an online training to learn more about how Webinars work.

ONLINE MARKETING

SIMON WALLACE-JONES

Simon Wallace-Jones started his Digital Marketing career in the late 80's implementing solutions for companies like DEC, Sun and Tektronix.

In 1996 he co-founded the pioneering company Relayware.com with his wife Louise, to develop one of the world's first enterprise-level, web-based, marketing automation solutions which is still in use today by leading brands like Sony, Lexmark and Lenovo. This solution pre-dated SalesForce.com and other leaders like Infusionsoft.

After successfully exiting their first company in 2008 he and Louise co-founded Oxford Digital Marketing to help smaller businesses take their use of Digital Marketing to the next level.

He believes Digital Marketing skills should be part of a core set of business knowledge and is passionate about empowering people to be able to use them. He is actively passing on the knowledge and experience he has gained through pioneering web-based marketing with some of the worlds leading brands.

SOCIAL MEDIA
BUTTONS
3 STEPS TO UNLEASH
AN ARMY OF VOLUNTEER MARKETERS

Simon is a highly skilled and highly sort after Digital Marketing Expert who has added huge value to the members of my Oxford Business Wealth Club where he's a vibrant member.

I've also had the pleasure of coaching him and his wife Louise and I can tell you they have a powerful Vision to help business owners, just like you, harness the power of digital tools such as Wordpress, SEO, Infusionsoft and Social Media to name a few.

Their monthly workshops receive rave reviews and I've sent several of my team, and my clients on them to fast track their knowledge and skills in these areas. Their feedback is always 10 out of 10 for content, business value and enjoyment.

Simon also has the brilliant skill of being able to help you Automate your Marketing Systems in the business to remove pressure points, generate more sales and grow your profits. He's currently my "go to man" for everything involving Infusionsoft, and it's already paying big dividends.

— *Paul Avins*

> Over the last few years, companies like Facebook, LinkedIn, Twitter and most recently Google have handed us a set of simple tools which, if set up correctly, can unleash an army of volunteers to help our marketing efforts with minimal to zero effort from us.

Social Media voting buttons are all over the web and yet most of the business people I speak to do not know what most of them are or why they should care.

In this chapter I'm going to show you a simple three step process you can follow to have your friends, customers, business parters and website visitors spread the word for you about your business or services for free.

The moment a customer clicks one of these buttons on your web page, your content can be in front of hundreds of new people. If the content or product your customer has promoted is good, a portion of their contacts can become new customers for you.

I understand you may be skeptical. Your experience may have been that when you click a button, it simply goes into the void of the Internet.

How can you prove this stuff is worth the effort? The only guarantees I can make are:

- To make it work you have to have these buttons in place on your web pages.

- It will only work if you educate your visitors, customers, friends and business partners to click the buttons.

- It will cost very little to implement with potentially significant and continuous returns.

The research shows that visitors don't click these buttons for two primary reasons:

- Some people are nervous to click the buttons because they don't know what happens when they do.

- Website owners are not asking their visitors to click the buttons clearly enough.

It's easy to deal with both of these reasons with a simple explanation and a clear call to action.

Any business person who does a lot of face-to-face networking will tell you that they get business by regularly turning up to meetings, not necessarily directly from the meetings themselves. The more you turn up, the more it increases your chances of doing business. A few weeks ago I attended a networking breakfast and completely out of the blue, came away with over a thousand pounds worth of business.

Consistent action delivers results!

By encouraging and educating your customers to click their favourite button, you are doing something similar. You are increasing your chances of having your brand and messages put in front of more people.

THREE STEPS TO MAKE THEM WORK FOR YOU

Below I have outlined a simple 3 step process of making these buttons work for you.

1. Choose which of the buttons are likely to put your content in front of the right audience. (I'll describe the audiences you can expect from each shortly.)

2. Implement them on your blog and product pages.

3. Educate your customers, visitors and partners to click on the buttons.

Lets first spend a few moments looking at each of the big five buttons in turn.

ONLINE MARKETING

137

1,202 ▼Tweet TWITTER'S TWEET BUTTON

Twitter's Tweet button is very popular with people who like to tweet so it is a no-brainer to add it to your web pages because a portion of your visitors will be Twitter users.

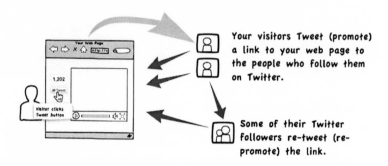

WHO DOES IT REACH?

It reaches the people who follow your visitors on Twitter. This will be a good thing particularly if these are your customers, as often their Twitter followers will be like minded people who could be ideal customers for you. If it gets re-Tweeted the content can go to followers of followers and can get picked up by journalists and other amplifiers who have a huge Twitter following.

♡482 f Like FACEBOOK'S LIKE BUTTON

Facebook's Like button is probably the most well known because of Facebook's huge user base. Also the use of the thumbs up symbol as it's primary icon makes it very intuitive to click.

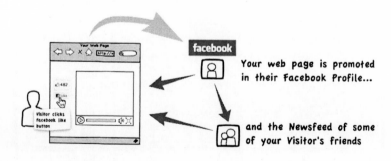

WHO DOES IT REACH?

It reaches some of your visitors Friends on Facebook. If you are selling to people in their personal life, then this will work well. Earlier in 2011 Facebook published statistics showing consumer-facing companies Like Levis, were experiencing a 40% increase in traffic coming to their website from Facebook after the Like buttons were installed.

For pure business-to-business marketing, this can be less effective, unless you are using it for developing your brand in the community.

274 — LINKEDIN'S **SHARE BUTTON**

The LinkedIn Share button was launched in Nov 2010. LinkedIn has more that 120 million, mostly professional users and its growth is rampant. UK LinkedIn users went from 4 million to more than 6 million in the last year.

WHAT HAPPENS WHEN YOUR VISITORS CLICK IT?

When they promote your content, it goes out on their updates and this can reach your visitor's most active contacts on LinkedIn. If they also promote your material to a LinkedIn Group, it will reach all of the group members.

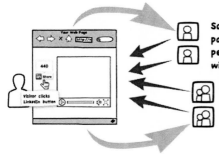

Some visitors will promote your page to LinkedIn. Some of the people they are connected to will click through to your page.

Some visitors will promote your page to their LinkedIn Groups. Interested group members will click through to your page.

WHO DOES IT REACH?

If you are selling your products and services to business people, academics and senior management then LinkedIn is an essential place to target. If you can encourage your customers and visitors to click for you, you will see more traffic coming from LinkedIn as a result.

ONLINE MARKETING

GOOGLE'S +1 BUTTON

Google's +1 button (launched in April 2011) may become the most effective button for many small businesses. When a user clicks the +1 button on your piece of content, they are promoting it to their friends and contacts. This happens both in Google's search results and inside the new Google+.

(Google+ at the time of writing is in a runaway success beta phase. Assuming it rolls out, it is easy to see how 300-400 million people will become users of Google+ almost overnight, just by Google converting a portion of the 100's of millions of users.)

WHAT HAPPENS WHEN YOUR VISITORS CLICK IT?

Adding the +1 button to your pages lets your visitors recommend your content, knowing that their friends and contacts will see their recommendation when it's most relevant—in the Google search results!

WHO DOES IT REACH?

This is the exciting thing about the +1 button. If a visitor has clicked the +1 on your web page, when a connection of theirs is signed-in and searching Google, a relevant search result will show a highlighted +1 button and your visitor's picture and your page will appear higher in the search results for that user.

For example, when searching for cheap startup logo, my search results showed that a friend of mine has shared this (as in the graphic below).

The quest for a cheap startup logo | Simpleweb
simpleweb.co.uk/2011/the-quest-for-a-cheap-startup-logo/ - Cached
2 Aug 2011 – **The quest for a cheap startup logo**. Tweet. I've been hearing a lot about
99designs over the last year or so. I've found it difficult to give ...
Tom Holder shared this

If a searcher is logged in but not directly connected to your visitor, they will simply see that some people have clicked +1 on your page in the search results.

STUMBLEUPON'S STUMBLE BUTTON

StumbleUpon's Stumble button is less well known however gs.statcounter.com shows that 15 million users on StumbleUpon send the second highest volume of traffic to websites after Facebook.

StumbleUpon is a discovery engine that allows you to find and recommend websites of interest. If you create good enough content and people give it the thumbs up on StumbleUpon, your content and brand will likely appear from time-to-time in front of other users.

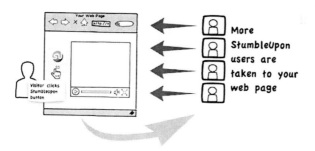

More StumbleUpon users are taken to your web page

Visitor clicks StumbleUpon button

WHO DOES IT REACH?

StumbleUpon is especially attractive to consumer market niches especially including: travel and tourism, photography, boating, astronomy, music and design.

HOW DO I ADD THE BUTTONS TO MY SITE?

Each of the buttons are added by going to the relevant pages on Google, Twitter, Facebook, LinkedIn and StumbleUpon and copying and pasting the appropriate lines of code into the correct place on your website code.

I realise that you may be thinking well where is 'the correct place on my website code'? The answer will depend on how you have implemented your website. I'll answer for four common scenarios.

1. If you manage your own website and know how to edit the code yourself, then you'll simply need to go to the relevant configuration pages provided by Google, Twitter, Facebook, LinkedIn and StumbleUpon and fill out some simple details to get your lines of code to paste.

2. If you run your website on WordPress, you can choose from a number of plugins like Slick Social Share Buttons, Add This or Sexy Bookmarks to achieve the result very easily.

3. If you are using another Content Management System, you'll have to either talk to your supplier or if it's a popular system, they may already have a solution like WordPress plugins.

4. If your website is managed by someone else then you can give them the link and the installation instructions below for the details on how to sort it out for you.

I love zero cost ideas

For more details on how to add social media buttons for your site follow this link http://odmtips.com/installing-buttons

The best news is that the implementation costs will be anything from zero to the cost of a couple of hours of your web person's time.

EDUCATING YOUR VOLUNTEER PROMOTIONAL ARMY

OK so you've installed these on your website, now what? Now you've got to encourage your visitors to click them.

If the buttons are on blog posts, make sure they show at the top and bottom of the post. To make these buttons work effectively, you need to challenge yourself or your business to get into the habit of producing good quality content. Content that people are going to want to praise and share by clicking it. A tip here is that visual and video based content is more appealing and tends to get more clicks.

I like to add a box at the end of my blog posts which tells the reader what to do next.

If you have buttons on your product pages, add an email auto-responder sequence to your post-purchase follow-up which asks your customers to share about their experience with their connections on one or more of the networks. We regularly have people who come on our trainings as a direct result of reading a tweet a previous delegate has made.

Just like all sales coaches teach you to ask for referrals, you want to be educating your visitors, customers and friends in the mantra "If you like our stuff, click our buttons".

NEXT STEPS

If you've not implemented all of the relevant buttons on your web pages and would like to find out more about how to implement them, then please go to

www.odmtips.com/installing-buttons

If you have already implemented them, let me encourage you to sign-up for our free Digital Marketing tips at:

www.odmtips.com/wealth-accelerators

ONLINE MARKETING

SIMON K WILLIAMS

Simon K Williams is better known as The App Man, he is the author of the acclaimed book *Rich App Poor App*, and through his seminars, events, and products has helped thousands of people across four continents discover their unique app-ortunities, and developed those initial ideas into commercially successful applications.

His background is in commercial design, with 17 years of experience and has a client list that includes Virgin, American Express, and Sony to name a few.

He has simply transferred the proven three-step product creation formula he developed as a Product and Service Designer over to the mobile App environment.

"I know that everyone has the ability to make a Million Dollar App but they need some help to make that happen – and that's where I step in. We take care of them throughout the entire journey making sure they avoid any potential pitfalls, to ensure their success."

HOW TO PROFIT FROM
MOBILE APPS

I've known Simon for a while now through the Speaking Circuit - and when we met up again recently at Dr Joanna Martin's 3 day Presentation Profits course he gave me a copy of his new book, Rich App Poor App. (What a great twist on a classic book title).

So when I started to think about an App for The Business Wealth Club, he was my first phone call. I have to say that I really did enjoy reading his book - it's one that I always have handy in my library for any clients who need to learn about the world of sales via Apps... as you are about to now!

— *Paul Avins*

> Consumers have changed the way they buy, have you changed the way you sell?

I became acutely aware that there was a significant and profound change in consumer behaviour after producing a 30,000 word academic paper on the subject in 2007. In a nutshell what I discovered was a profound and sustained 'shift' away from physical products, towards highly emotive, highly niche solutions.

This knowledge changed my life, will either make or break your business, and is changing the way we do business forever.

NEEDS OF THE HEART...

Over the course of many centuries society has moved from the **needs of the stomach**, which led to the agrarian age (farming). The **needs of the brain**, which led to the industrial age and the service industry. To the **needs of the heart**, which is the era of society we are now immersed in, which I call, The Emotional Age.

Here are three examples of The Emotional Age in action;

Big Brother: Not on our TV screens now, but big brother changed TV forever.

Instead of providing traditional entertainment, Big Brother instead delivered a psychological or emotional product. This phenomenon was Worldwide earning Endemol over £600 million per year in profits.

Amazon: Not merely a bookshop online. Amazon's success is down to what's called the long tail phenomenon. If you're not familiar with this term, it simply means that there are more people buying more unique, and nearly unique products than ever before.

Amazon make more money, not from the big blockbuster book titles we all know such as Harry Potter, but actually from the obscure titles we have never heard of. Amazon actually makes more profit

Now isn't that interesting...!

from the titles outside their top 100,000 best sellers than they do in it! That is a massive shift in consumer behaviour.

Last but certainly not least, and perhaps the most obvious, and definitely the most recent is... The mobile App market...

Mobile Apps: On Thursday July 10th 2008, a certain computer company called Apple launched an intriguing service called the App Store. It allowed real everyday people to produce, sell, and buy products on practically any subject imaginable.

MASSIVE GROWTH

In just the first nine short months, Apple announced over one billion Apps had been downloaded. At the time of writing over 16 billions Apps have been downloaded from the Apple platform alone, and the rate of growth is higher now than it's ever been.

To use one high profile example, the Angry Birds App has generated 10's of millions of pounds in profit, from what is essentially a simple but well executed game. Such is the power of this App, that it has now been expanded into a Hollywood movie no less.

Even a super-simple App like Night-Stand which is a clock and alarm clock originally created just for the iPad made over $20,000 in profit in just it's first three weeks on sale. And this was when the iPad was only on sale in one country, it now sells across 97 countries.

THEORY

Bakhtin the Russian philosopher, who is regarded by many as one of the most important theorists of literature and culture, believed that every person had a need for individuality; he said "Because I am actual and irreplaceable I must actualize my uniqueness". Mobile applications fulfil this powerful desire, they...

Allow regular individuals (not just organisations), to create powerful, unique packages of information, knowledge, and entertainment on practically any subject or niche, and to distribute these creations across the globe through an entirely 100% digital distribution channel.

These solutions have the opportunity to engage in highly emotive ways, tapping into the senses of touch, (through the unique interactions of gestures that these smart devices employ), sound, and of course vision. In many ways these are the most emotive products our society has ever produced.

TIME TO JUMP

Given my knowledge of this change in consumer behaviour, it's little surprise that I jumped aboard the App phenomenon as soon as I could. I quit my full time work just four months after launching my very first App, thanks completely to the passive revenue that I was now enjoying.

This has allowed me to take control of my life, to travel, and to launch my own Company called AppManSecrets, which helps others share in this great opportunity.

Everybody has the power and the opportunity to create their very own App, you don't need any experience, you don't need any IT skills, you don't even need to own a mobile phone.

I have now helped thousands of people understand the power of this emerging and powerful media format, which have delivered through seminars across four continents so far.

I'd call that Expert Positioning!

I am also the published Author of *Rich App Poor App*, which explains how you can maximize this amazing opportunity for yourself. My team and I have produced well over 100 mobile applications across over 30 different industries, which makes us one of the most prolific App creators in the UK today.

APP ROOKIE MISTAKES

Here is my list of the 7 most common App Rookie mistakes in reverse order; avoid these and you will be well on your way to a mega-selling commercial App-ortunity. We will make sure you don't fall into any of these potential pitfalls...

1. Don't have a strategy to ensure positive user reviews on the App store...

2. Don't check for competition...

3. Don't protect your concept...

4. Don't know how to test your concept...

5. Don't get expert advice...

6. Procrastinate, and watch others beat you to your market...

7. Rely on a developer to turn their idea into a commercial product...

Developers get paid to code, that's what they do. They do what they are told, keep you happy, get paid, and move on. You need to test before you build, we can show you how, read the Paul Avins Special Bonus below...

NEXT STEPS

If you want to discover what your million pound App idea is, how to test your concept, or just want to learn more about this exciting and expanding industry, then we have a great Bonus just for you...

- *Free chapters from the acclaimed Rich App Poor App book*

  So you can learn the facts about the industry!

- *Free invitation to join our next online seminar (subject to availability)*

  Get all your questions answered!

- *Free Non Disclosure Agreement*

  (So no one else can get rich from your ideas!)

Go now to:

www.AppManSecrets.com/PaulAvinsBonus.html

ONLINE MARKETING

TODAY IN ALL AREAS OF LIFE, BUSINESS PEOPLE ARE LOOKING TO EXPERTS TO HELP THEM MAKE MONEY, GROW THEIR BUSINESS AND ACHIEVE THEIR GOALS. THIS HAS CREATED AN EXPERT INDUSTRY AND WE'LL SHOW YOU HOW TO TAP IN...

EXPER
POSIT

T
ONING

HELENA HOLRICK

Helena Holrick has been in the Learning and Development arena for over 25 years. She has designed and delivered presentations and workshops for thousands of people across many industries, focused on skill development, productivity, management and leadership.

On one project she is particularly proud of, she delivered Performance Management training to 1,300 people over 9 months at the London Fire Brigade, across all levels of the organisation up to The Board and Assistant Director.

Helena's passion is helping people shine as she is a true Supporter.

Her commitment, encouragement, energy and enthusiasm fuel her desire to create great results for clients and businesses through her one to one Mentoring, and as the Business Wealth Club Mentor for Croydon.

Her appetite for growing, connecting and shifting people combined with her love of learning means that she continues to invest heavily her own growth (she is a Clean Language Facilitator, NLP Master Practitioner, Action Learning Set Facilitator, Master Coach, and is completing a level 5 Coaching and Mentoring Diploma with CMI). These are just some of the tools, techniques and coaching skills she employs to help others to achieve greater success.

HOW TO BE A WORKSHOP WIZARD

The Business Wealth Club Open Days attract amazing people, some of who get inspired to join our Community and their local Clubs - a few, like Helena see the Bigger Opportunity and set up to Mentor a club in their own Community!

I remember our conversation like it was yesterday:

Helena said "I see you don't have a Club in Croydon yet? When do you think you'll be launching one as I would like to join a club more local to me?"

My response "We don't have one planned yet so why don't you open one?" slight pause from Helena....."OK then I WILL!"

This whole conversation just shows the positive, can do attitude that she possesses and that members and mentors love to be around.

Her back ground in business and personal development, especially her event skills, which she's used to help another co-author in this book Dr Joanna Martin, set her up for success on a serious level.

You'll have to go a long way to meet somebody with such a big heart and the commercial brains and comprehension to back it up.

The fact that she had Members wanting to join her club before it officially launched is testimony to the magnetic energy she projects and that the Croydon Community well embodies.

— Paul Avins

> When you are easy to learn from, people not only remember what you say, they come back to you for more than they learned the first time. When your message is structured and delivered simply and cleanly and is supported by helpful ways to remember, your impact, income and influence soar.

MAKING YOUR IMPACT, INCOME AND INFLUENCE SOAR

I really want you to be your brilliant self. I want you to share what you know, what you've worked so hard to learn and discover, and I want you to do it in such a way that it inspires movement and action in others.

In this Chapter I'll cover a simple model that will help you distil the vast amount of ideas, experience and "stuff' you know and package it into a workshop, presentation or a 40 Second Networking pitch that will help you engage and entice your chosen audience so that you win more business.

You ARE Brilliant!

Because you're reading this book, it's likely you will recognise yourself: You are creative; you have a big heart and a great vision; you know a lot about something you really care about and you want to share it.

You inspire people with big ideas about reforming or transforming the way we live and enjoy life, the way we do business, make sales or serve customers.

You've probably got years of study, experience and knowledge that's crammed into your head and it's now at the stage where it's bubbling over and bursting to get 'out'. It may even be giving you sleepless nights!

When you are this passionate, the logical next step is to teach your information to people it can help and add value to. This can happen through running a workshop, delivering a talk, setting up a webinar or perhaps speaking at a Networking event as a guest speaker or trainer for an Industry body.

THE PROBLEM WITH BEING BRILLIANT...

In my experience of working with many brilliant people, the down side of being a 'Passionate Expert' is that until you learn how to shape your knowledge, you are likely to fall into the three traps when sharing your message with (smaller or large) groups of people. Often completely without realising it or meaning to:

● You are boring and a real turn off for the audience

● You can be a bit of a bully, delivering you information from a place of "I KNOW" you don't!

● You can come off as big-headed, especially in the more reserved cultures like the UK

● Or, worse of all – you achieve all three at the same time!

Getting active participation from your audience is vital – it keeps them engaged and keeps them learning!

Instead of inspiring action or giving people that one key piece that will transform their lives or businesses, you find your audience turns from you in confusion, boredom or lack of interest in ever working with you to help solve their problems. In short, you fail to achieve your desired goals on all levels!

THE GOOD NEWS: THERE IS HOPE AND HELP TO SHAPE YOUR BRILLIANCE AND YOUR MESSAGE...

I want to share with you the model I use when I coach my clients; it's called the 4Ease Model. This will help you sort what you need to say to keep your audience engaged, interested and more likely buying from you more often.

Through this proven structure and preparation technique, which takes very little time, you might just find you will be more fluid, flexible and authentic with your material than ever before, resulting in more opportunities to share your message, more leads and more business.

EXPERT POSITIONING

155

When creating content for anything, you first need to set some clear intentions and ask yourself the following questions

- Who is my audience and what are their issues?

- What do I want and need to tell them to add value? (and why)

- What can I share with them right now to help solve their No.1 issue?

For the purposes of this chapter, I am going to make an assumption that you already know what your Content is centred on. Now it's time to shape that content into the following flow sections:

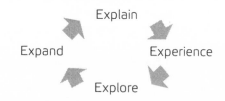

Explain

Expand

Experience

Explore

STEP 1 – EXPLAIN ("BUY IT")

Your Goal is to Create BUY IN....to You, Your Credibility, Your Message and Your Ability to Help them Solve a Problem in their Business or Life.

As you take to any stage or platform, you have to grab the audience's attention and get their buy-in straight away. The best way to do this is to pepper your first few sentences (or five minutes if you have longer) with lots of reasons for them to give you their attention. You do this by making it VERY relevant, having a good WIIFM (What's In It For Me) as well as promising a payoff for listening by heavily hinting that listening may just provide them with the solution they need right now.

- This section needs to answer the question "WHY should I listen to you?"

- Engage their Right Brain (Where the Emotional Centre Lives) with success stories that demonstrate benefits and desires the audience are likely to want for themselves

- Tell them relevant statistics and facts that grab, impress or compel their imagination

- Tell some 'opposite' stories (what they won't get if they don't pay attention)

- This bit is the EDUCATION of their (unconscious) needs

ACTIVATION EXERCISE:

Identify your topic information, and just let your brain identify 5-6 possible benefits in the following areas for your talk: Money/Wealth, Health/Well-being, Relationships/Friendship, Leadership/Strategies, Management/Support.

Now for each of your benefits, access your mind for examples of people you've worked with or in your wider circle who have gained these benefits as a result of what you are sharing or teaching.

Now that you have audience BUY IN, you can move on to the next section or part of your presentation.

STEP 2 – EXPERIENCE ("FEEL IT")

Your goal is to Engage and Entice this Listener...

As your talk or workshop opens up, you must build in an emotionally engaging experience with your audience, especially if you want them to buy anything from you when you've finished!! It's critical to touch their hearts and minds and allow them to connect with themselves and you.

You do this by:

- Telling true stories related to your subject – Facts Tell, Stories Sell... Your own story (Be sure to blend Your Humanity with Your Expertise) and the success stories of others you've helped (videos, audio clips work best)

- Reminding them through rhetorical questions about their own (good/bad) experiences in this area: e.g. "have you ever felt like everything was just on the edge of happening but you couldn't quite get to it?"

- A mini exercise, done in the mind or even on a piece of paper (e.g. listing pros/cons to highlight where they are currently at around the subject)

- You can bring in a little more about the subject through your stories – e.g. Mary attributes the success she's now experiencing now through learning these 4 key things…

- This section is about EDUCATION and ENGAGEMENT – it creates a full desire to actually hear about your topic

EXPERIENCE EXERCISE:
a. bring to mind 3 examples of people who've 'worked' your brand of brilliance and write their story or get a testimonial from them, and b. Write down three rhetorical questions that would help the audience recall a situation they would love to let go of / get out of.

Once the audience is FEELING IT, you can move them on to the next section.

STEP 3 - EXPLORE ("OWN IT")

Your goal is to help them understand your model or idea, and what it means for them in reality

By this part of your presentation, you should have permission and probably the desire in the audience to hear the core idea or model you want to share and to tell them a little about how it works. Once you have, you MUST help them actually work out how what you are saying will apply to them, specifically.

If you are doing a talk rather than a workshop, you need give them the outline of what your model is, explain to them how it works and what the parts are. Depending on your time available, you must help them understand how it applies to them through a short or long exercise:

- Present your model or idea in a step-by-step format, or present a bullet list of how it works as a model – then invite them to apply it then and there!

- Participation equals Sales so more exercises and less talking

- Allow them time to experiment, play and get familiar with the concept or technique you are wanting them to embrace

- The focus of this section is centred on HOW TO DO IT and own it for themselves (and in longer time frames, PRACTICE)

- This bit is MAKING YOUR KNOWLEDGE THEIRS (yes, I'm saying give it away, let them play!)

EXPLORE EXERCISE:
Come up with a mini-interview that could be done in pairs - 2 or 3 questions is enough – that helps them contextualise what you have presented, then give them the opportunity to speak those out loud to each other. (This is a great way to 'check the learning' and emphasise)

Once the audience OWN IT, you can move them on to the final consolidating section.

STEP 4 – EXPAND ("DO IT")

Your goal is to ask your audience to make a decision, set at least one action for themselves or commit to change

In this section, you get them to embrace the IMPACT of learning your model or idea and help them understand how they might actually use this directly in their lives or businesses.

Highlight and summarise the underlying concept (relaxation, efficiency, productivity etc.) and get them to work out where else this skill is useful to them or their clients:

- Get the audience to do a little more exploration, or get them discussing it together

- Get them to sell you on why they need to know it (use it also to summarise!)

- Finally get them to make a decision: is this useful to them, and if so how? Or is it something that was interesting to hear about but not relevant right now? If so, invite them to let it go completely so they are free to use the energy elsewhere.

- If they are engaged, and it's likely they will be, get them to make a commitment to use this in some way in the next 24 or 72 hours. Get them to set an ACTION.

- This section is all about MAKING THE MODEL / IDEA THEIRS and doing something with it

EXPAND EXERCISE:

Decide what you need to invite action on. Come up with key decisions your audience need to make and build this into your invitation. Be clear on the next steps you want them to take after you finish. Then invite them to take that step!

Once they DO IT, they are now on the road to increasing their Sales, Profits and Success and DOING SOMETHING more with your information and probably with you too – if you make them an offer!

GO OUT THERE AND BE BRILLIANT!

When you next need to sell an idea, share a model, give a talk or deliver a presentation, I invite you to use the BUY IT – FEEL IT – OWN IT – DO IT cycle of planning your content. It will make sure you use your knowledge and expertise to focus on giving them exactly what they want and need. You will usually find that the more they 'Do It', the more they 'Buy It' and that's how customer loyalty sets in… and do let me know how you get on!

NEXT STEPS

Helena Holrick is the Mentor for The Business Wealth Club in Croydon – to come along and experience her support and proven business building workshop visit www.thebusinesswealthclub.co.uk/Croydon today to claim 1 months Free Membership!

As well as supporting local businesses, she also works with people 121 to just get their information and experience out of their heads and into a structure and shape that suits and delights them and others.

Or if you love working through this kind of thing with others she regularly run webinars and workshops to kick start you on your next project(s). Find out more by connecting with her:

Send her an email to let me know how you get on: helena@jworkshopsthatwork.co.uk

www.workshopsthatwork.co.uk

Find her on:

Linkedin.com/in/helenaholrick

Facebook.com/helenaholrick Twitter/helenaholrick

http://pinterest.com/helenaholrick/

AYD
INSTONE

Ayd Instone is a Creative Director with 18 years experience of design and marketing in print and mulitmedia (including working on the design of Microsoft's intranet.) and yet has a degree in Physics and Physical Science, proving that creativity really is the blend of the left and right brains.

Today he works as a keynote motivational speaker (on the topics of Creativity and Thought Innovation), graphic artist, brand consultant and publisher.

Ayd has run his own branding and design company, Eldamar ltd for 10 years where he has designed global marketing campaigns for the likes of Oxford University Press, Macmillan Publishers and Oxfam among others. Ayd has created around 200 brand identities for various businesses large and small.

In 2009 he launched his publishing business *Sunmakers* for expert speakers, coaches, consultants and entrepreneurs to help brand, design and publish their expertise as information products. He is the author of five published books of his own including *Ding How to Have a Great Idea* and *Don't Tell the Dinosaurs (The Secrets of the Future)* and the forthcoming *The Kudos Effect*. He has designed and published a further 25 books for other authors – including this one!

EXPERTISE BRANDING
HOW TO SELL
WHEN YOU'RE NOT
IN THE ROOM

Ayd is truly a one off! His unique sense of style, design and creativity give him a radically different take on branding, imagery and product design. In fact he saved me from going to print with a very uninspiring first book cover and the rework after he got his hands on it was just amazing. Which book? Business SOS my first book and now this book as well.

He's been a proactive member of *The Business Wealth Club* now since 2009 – and his 40 second networking songs are legendary! We've also worked together on several Stages working for clients in the motor industry and salon industry and audiences just love his guitar based keynote presentations! If any of my clients need support with producing their books to achieve expert positioning, I tell them they have no choice – they have to work with Ayd and many of them in this book already have.

— Paul Avins

> You must have heard the news by now, it's so extraordinary. In July 2011 it was revealed that Apple Inc. had more cash to spend than the United States government.

Figures from the US Treasury Department showed that the country had an operating cash balance of $73.7bn (£45.3bn) while Apple, with a net income 125% higher than their previous year, had $76.4bn sitting in the bank. This news follows over five years of consistent record breaking profits for Apple, overtaking long term rivals Microsoft in 2010 and in August 2011 overtook ExxonMobil to become the most valuable (and most powerful) company in the world.

So how did they do it? From being a company on its knees in 1995 and almost broke, how did they win over so many people, dominate so many markets and make so much money?

We could make a list of a great many clever business practices, but I want to focus on just one, which I believe to be a key one, because it's the only one that Apple does, and does well, that everyone else does badly or not at all. It's their understanding and implementation of branding and design. Apple's CEO, Steve Jobs, has always maintained that good design is central to Apple's purpose.

> *"In most people's vocabularies, design means veneer. It's interior decorating. It's the fabric of the curtains of the sofa. But to me, nothing could be further from the meaning of design. Design is not just what it looks like and feels like. Design is how it works." — Steve Jobs*

Apple incorporates great design into every aspect of its business; the products, the software, the online delivery services, the packaging and the marketing. To Apple, great design is their brand and that's what gives it its power.

If you bought an iPhone, think back to when you opened that box for the first time, you know what I'm talking about.

BUT WHAT IS A BRAND?

Imagine a farmer who has a field of cows. Not so far away is another farmer who also has cows. To anyone who isn't a cow expert, one cow looks pretty much like another, so the farmers decide to put marks on their cows so they know which ones belong to them to avoid any confusion. The mark differentiates them when they come to market.

If you were to come upon a cow in a field and perhaps fancied yourself as a bit of a rustler, and it looks like the coast is clear, you could easily make off with one of these cows. But once you notice the symbol on its hide you realise that you couldn't pass the cow off as your own. Not only that, you recognise the brand. It belongs to a particular farmer who wouldn't hesitate to shoot anyone who stole one of his cows. The values of the farmer have been transferred to the cow through the brand. You decide to leave the cow alone and move on.

This is the beginning of branding and this is how most companies and experts think it still works. They're wrong.

They're taking branding at its most simplistic form, something that differentiates items at market and encapsulates the values of its master through use of a simple symbol. So many businesses have got stuck at this shallow level. Their concept of branding only goes skin deep.

Part of the reason is to do with the rise of so-called Personal Branding. That is all about you and who you are, your reputation. Some business leaders have misunderstood the concept and have got sidetracked into fussing about wearing a particular coloured tie. They've started thinking about it all from the wrong side, adding constraints or veneers to themselves in an attempt to tattoo themselves just like the old cow.

21st century branding is not about having a veneer, or lip-gloss, something that covers over the cracks. It's not about surface anymore. Let's have another quote.

> *"Design is the fundamental soul of a human-made creation, that ends up expressing itself in successive outer layers of the product or service."* — *Steve Jobs*

New branding is about revealing that design. Your brand is not the name on the door but the name that goes through every part of the business like the name through a stick of rock. When I work with business leaders and experts, whether it's creating their visual identity or the design of their book, it's not about creating them a badge, or slapping a picture on the book cover. It's about revealing their inner light, their uniqueness, their offer, who they really are, who they have been all along and letting the light of their expertise shine. That's the real brand (that, incidentally is why my company is called Sunmakers.)

My job is to make this brand visible and the result we get I call your **Expertise Brand**. Your Expertise Branding is the look of the 'stuff' that continues to sell for you when you're not in the room. It is the marketing materials or products that need no introduction or explanation because they encapsulate the message.

Take Action – complete this section for yourself now!

If Personal Branding is what people SAY when you're not there, Expertise Branding is what people will PAY when you're not there. It's about what you do, what you provide for your clients. To better define your brand, you need to know where you stand. Here are some positioning questions. Answer them in sentences.

1. **What exactly are you selling and who is the target audience?**

   ....

   ....

2. **Why is it worth it? What pain and problems does it solve?**

   ....

   ....

3. Who are you and why should anyone believe you?

....

....

4. Who are your competitors and how are you different from them?

....

....

5. What objections would potential clients have to using your services, products or message?

....

....

....

6. Where is your current branding shown (stationery, website, signs, products)? Are they consistent? Do they reflect where you are today or where you were yesterday?

....

....

....

7. What are the key words associated with your business?

....

....

8. If your business was a car, what car would it be? What animal would it be? If it was a restaurant, what style of food would be on the menu?

....

....

....

EXPERT POSITIONING

9. What is your expertise story? What were the ups and downs and turning points that got you to where you are? What lessons did you learn?

....

....

....

10. Why does your business exist? (In addition to making a profit) What is the big reason why?

....

....

This is your vision statement. It should be far-reaching and universal.

Items that carry your Expertise Brand can be passed from the person you gave them to, to someone else who you may never have met, perhaps the decision maker – without losing any part of the essence of the brand through degradation or misunderstandings and without lessening enthusiasm and connection. Expertise Branding allows your brand message to be continuously re-broadcast fresh from your physical materials without explanation, delivering a powerful impact.

Many consultant experts and business leaders spend years building up their reputation only to have it dashed by weak or badly designed products and materials that undermine client confidence in an instant. Don't let poor deliverables destroy your reputation.

You can judge this one, it's great!

It's often said, *don't judge a book by its cover*, but everyone does, and rightly so. If that's all we have to go on, we have to make a judgement by it. From most people's experience, things that look rubbish, usually are. Things that are presented badly, usually are. So if your offering looks amateur, it's quite reasonable for people to think that you are amateur, and you won't be able to charge Expert Prices either!

You can't blame them for it. If your business cards are those free ones, they will assume that you're not willing to invest in your business and don't value their potential custom. So they won't value or invest in you. If your book looks like the church magazine, done on the cheap, badly typeset with a cover that looks like a home made freebook, why should anyone pay your inflated day rate? In fact, why should they pay you at all?

Apple's secret is that they developed their brand using great design to create products and services that were previously regarded by their users and competitors as commodities. It was great design that lifted desktop PCs out of utilitarian beige into desirable status symbols whilst still being powerful and yet simple to use tools that even the most non-technical users could get the most out of. They re-invented the music and phone industries and will soon attempt to do the same with publishing and television. When you have an Expertise Brand you no longer offer a commodity. You no longer have to compete on price. You can dominate markets or even create them as Apple have done with the iPad, a device that nobody needed but everyone finds a use for.

Being good isn't enough. Looking good isn't enough. Create an Expertise Brand that reveals both by making great design part of your brand at every level and you too will be enjoying record sales and profits.

NEXT STEPS

*Get your **FREE** ebook on Expertise Branding and tips on turning your story into a published book that will enhance your expertise and help increase your fees and profits by visiting here:*

www.sunmakers.co.uk/wealthaccelerators.html

www.twitter.com/aydinstone
www.facebook.com/aydinstone
www.linkedin.com/in/aydinstone
skype: aydinstone

EXPERT POSITIONING

JOANNA MARTIN

Joanna graduated with 1st class honors after 6 years of medical school at the University of Tasmania but left medicine to take a position at the prestigious Actors Centre Australia, a forward thinking drama school, which introduced her to the field of personal development. Before long she was consulting to companies such as ANZ bank, John Fairfax Publishing and Ebay.

She was invited by Christopher Howard to take on the role of Head of Research and Training for his organisation and spent thousands of hours on the

stage perfecting her skills as a public speaker, educator and seminar sales person in front of tens of thousands of participants on three different continents. She then turned these skills into systems which were taught to new trainers so they could deliver similar results.

Joanna and her husband Greg have a number of information marketing businesses. One of the most well known of these is www.SecretsOfSellingFromStage.com where she teaches business owners the steps she used to make $1.25 million in her first 12 months as a professional speaker. The business dearest to her heart is *Shift Lifestyle* a resource created specifically for business owners who want to live life on their terms.

She is the co-author of the bestseller *Our Internet Secrets* and is about to release a new book, The Wealth Garden. Currently she is working on her third book, *The Lifestyle Shift* which will be available soon.

HOW TO USE SPEAKING
TO GROW YOUR BUSINESS PROFILE AND YOUR PROFITS

I was first introduced to Jo by Peter Thompson who told me that if I wanted to learn to take my platform skills to the next level, I had to attend her 3 day course - *Presentation Profits Intensive*. I'm glad I did!

Not only did her system have a dramatic impact on my business results, helping me close over £100,000 of Master Mind Coaching Contracts in just 2 hours from stage - but we've become friends as we share the same values and desire to make a difference in the world.

I recently went back on her course for a second time as I believe that repetition leads to Mastery..... so I suggest you read her chapter more than once!

— *Paul Avins*

> **Nothing I know has the power to accelerate your business faster than building your profile as a speaker.**

Speaking is my No. 1 marketing strategy

In fact, in my first 12 months as a speaker I was able to make over $1.25 million dollars in sales. And one of my students, made £207,000 in a weekend from 25 clients. How? Through the delivery of an "Effective Presentation."

Giving you an instant boost in credibility and celebrity, speaking will position you as the expert in your industry- and we all know that in uncertain times we all turn to the experts for advice. But many people can show you how to "give a good talk". I believe every speaking opportunity is the opportunity to get a new client. It is this mindset and strategy that has allowed me to build my own 7 figure income. So in this brief chapter I'll give you an overview of how to put together an Effective Presentation - which inspires your audience to take action at the end.

Let's get started.

There are *7 Key Elements to an Effective Presentation*.

You need all of them to get the result.

CREATE CONNECTION

In the first 2 minutes you spend on stage you must ENGAGE THE WHOLE ROOM. Do this by one or more of the following:

● Ask enrolling questions

● Engage them in an activity

● Tell a GOOD joke

● Blow them away with facts and stats

2 GET PERMISSION TO DO YOUR THING

You must get permission from your audience to speak to them, and ultimately to sell to them too. There are four key elements to this step:

EXPLAIN YOUR STYLE

For example I always make a point of telling my audience we'll be having a bit of fun while we learn as I tend to be a bit crazy on stage from time to time!

It doesn't matter what style you use in your presentation, as long as you outline it up front, tell them why you are that way, and then get on with it!

CONFIRM YOUR POSITION AS THE EXPERT

The key here is your credibility statement. Why on earth should these people bother to listen to you? Things to think about:

- What specific results have you achieved that prove your credibility?
- Have you got any testimonials that prove your credibility?
- Have you written a book?
- Do you have a Product / Media Coverage?

TELL THEM WHAT YOU ARE GOING TO TEACH

It makes good teaching sense to give your audience an overview of the steps of formula you are going to teach.

ASK PERMISSION FOR THE SALE

If you ask permission, your audience will unconsciously respond like a friend, and sit up and take notice.

Do not overtly tell them you are going to sell something. Instead get permission to "give them an opportunity" at the end of your talk.

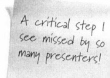

A critical step I see missed by so many presenters!

ENGAGE WITH YOUR CONTENT

This is the part of the presentation when you should teach something. Deliver value. So when designing the backbone of your presentation there are some key things to remember.

1. **Who are your audience and what level of expertise do they have in your field?** Ask yourself the following questions and design your backbone to deliver what they want:

   - Who are your audience?

   - What level of experience do they have?

   - What are their needs, wants, fears and frustrations?

   - What's their biggest problem?

   - What's their greatest dream?

2. **Create your content so it sells your product.** Make sure the topic is related to the sale you want to make.

3. **Create the backbone so that it fits easily into your time restrictions**. Remember you'll need about 5-10% of the time to create connection and build raport with your opening. And your offer will take another 10-15% of the total time. I advise that you stick to 3-5 key points in total for a 60-90 minute presentation. More than that can get overwhelming.

4. **Use testimonials to back up the value of the points you're teaching.**

4 ESTABLISH NEED

Ultimately your goal in this part is *TO CREATE TENSION BETWEEN WHERE THEY ARE AND WHERE THEY WANT TO BE.*

Do this by digging up their pain, and painting a bright vision of the future for them using emotional language.

5 REVEAL YOUR PRODUCT, SERVICE OR SOLUTION...

Things to think about when designing your offer:

- Who is your audience and what is it they want from you?

- What price point is reasonable based on what you know of your audience?

- What is the central product: is it CDs, DVDs, books, consumer products, seminars, consulting, other services, or a mix?

- What bonuses could you add to build the value?

- Could you make a two-tiered product offering, perhaps a basic version of your pack and a deluxe version with an extra special bonus or two?

WHEN REVEALING THE PRODUCT CONTINUE TO BUILD TENSION

By this stage in your presentation your audience will be aware of the fact that they are not getting the results they deserve.

EXPERT POSITIONING

175

This segment is the beginning of the close. During this segment you can introduce:

- Why you created your product.

- What your product is called.

- Who it's for.

- Who it's not for.

- A benefit-focused description of what it does *AND WHAT IT INCLUDES*.

- Proof of what you say is true with further testimonials if needed.

> **WARNING: I see seasoned professionals who are gifted entertainers turn into stilted robots when it comes to introducing the product. It is ESSENTIAL that you deliver this part of the presentation with just as much emotion and passion as you did the backbone.**

6 MAKE YOUR NO-BRAINER OFFER

Your next job is to give them a reason to buy NOW. Give them a reason WHY to buy and use the LAW OF SCARCITY.

People want what they can't have. So when designing your offer think about what "limiter" you can put on it. I'm a great believer in TELLING THE TRUTH. So... make sure you always endorse this with...

GUARANTEE

What guarantee can you make on your product or service that removes all risk for the customer? The bigger and bolder the guarantee the more you will sell.

7 INVITE IMMEDIATE ACTION

Once you've outlined and inspired people with your offer you have to tell them exactly what to do.

NEXT STEPS

These 7 simple steps can make a significant impact to your bottom line when applied. Not only that, but by becoming the speaker on a topic, your credibility and celebrity will skyrocket. And that will help you to get a stream of warm leads into your business.

For more detail on these 7-Steps and to get some free support in putting your presentation together, visit my website:

www.shiftspeakertraining.com/wealthclub

EXPERT POSITIONING

DANIEL
PRIESTLEY

In 2006 armed with little more than a suitcase and a credit card, Daniel arrived in London and began using online tools to build a network of clients, suppliers, partners and team. That business is Triumphant Events.

In little over two years the business achieved more than 40,000 bookings from over 850 affiliated marketing partners. Daniel is considered to be a leader in the application of Social Media and Affiliate Marketing in a small business.

As Triumphant Events UK keeps expanding and growing, Daniel is in constant demand around the world. He speaks to audiences throughout Asia, Australia, Europe and the United States and his topics include: Marketing, Social Media, Affiliate Marketing and Entrepreneurial Leadership.

Daniel is also passionate about social entrepreneurship and is a business advisor to Global Angels (www.globalangels.org). He is also a long time supporter of StepUP Foundation (www.stepupfoundation.com) and is attending the 30th annual summit for "The Hunger Project".

HOW TO BECOME A KEY PERSON OF INFLUENCE IN YOUR INDUSTRY IN THE NEXT 6 MONTHS

My first interaction with Daniel was at the Make It Big Conference in 2010 his company, Triumphant Events, had asked me to speak. I was instantly impressed with his passion and desire to help business owners and entrepreneurs succeed through Social Media. We hit it off and became friends and so I made it my business to get him along to one of our legendary Business Wealth Club Open Days so that our Members could get key insights in this important area of marketing.

Following on from that success, Daniel spoke for my Motor Industry Master Mind Group (available on DVD) - and we have gave his first book, *How to Become a Key Person of Influence*, to all our Club Members and Mentors as a book of the month.

He's great live - and I know you're going to get value from his chapter here in Wealth Accelerators...

— *Paul Avins*

> In any industry there are *Key People of Influence*
>
> Their names come up in conversation
> ... *for all the right reasons*
>
> They attract a lot of opportunities
> ... *the right sort*
>
> They earn a lot more money than most people
> ... *and it isn't a struggle*
>
> They can make something successful if they are
> involved ...*and people know it*

Key People enjoy a special status in their chosen field because they are well connected, well known, well regarded and highly valued. They get invited to be a part of the best teams and projects; and they can often write their own terms.

Key People of Influence also have more fun. They get invited on trips away, people buy them dinner and drinks, they are treated with respect and others listen when they speak.

People think that it must take years or decades to become a Key Person of Influence (KPI). They think that KPI's need degrees or doctorates. They think KPI's must be gifted or from a wealthy family.

While time invested, qualifications, talents and a wealthy family are helpful, they aren't a reliable way to make yourself a KPI.

There are plenty of people who have been in an industry for years who are NOT a Key Person of Influence. There are plenty of MBA's and Ph.d's who are NOT a KPI. There are talented people and people born in the right families who aren't either.

And then there are the strange stories like mine.

I arrived in the UK with nothing more than a suitcase and a credit card in 2006. I knew no one and I didn't have a lot of money.

Within 3 years, people started calling me one of the most connected entrepreneurs in London. I had built a business turning over millions and I could get on the phone to all of the big heavy hitters in my industry within a few calls.

All this in London. A city that is known for being a closed shop, full of "Old-Boys Networks". I was told that it wouldn't be possible to crack into the "Establishment" and I wouldn't be able to network "above my station".

How very wrong they were. It's not difficult to become a KPI in any industry in 6 months. But you have to do the things set out below, you have to do them well and you must do them in order. If you do, you won't need to do more University or spend decades climbing ladders; you will rapidly become a Key Person of Influence in your field.

How do you become a "Key Person"... faster?

It's surprisingly easy to become recognised as a Key Person if you take the time to put these five things in place...

---

1 YOU NEED TO KNOW YOUR NICHE & YOUR MICRO-NICHE

It's not enough to have a niche. You need a niche within a niche. When you have that, you tend to answer the question "what do you do?" with a lot more authority and power. A niche is "Bodybuilding" a micro-niche is "Vegetarian Bodybuilding" or "12 Week Transformations" or

Clarity is key!

"Christian Bodybuilding in the M25". When you know exactly the specific game that you're playing you don't just make more money, you also have more fun and see more rewards.

2 YOU NEED A BOOK

This isn't hard. It will take you 6 months (tops) from the day you sit and jot down your concept to the day you open up a brown box full of books with your face on them.

These days you can publish very short runs of books (you could start by ordering 20 copies of your book) and it's easy to get it up on Amazon. A few shining reviews (from people who share the same names of people who frequent your dinner parties) and all of a sudden you are a published author with global distribution.

3 YOU NEED A PRODUCT

Not difficult either. A day with a voice recorder (and no kids in the background), a few quid spent with an audio guy to "top and tail" it and then it's ready for manufacture. You'll spend about £1 per copy for a boxed CD or DVD and once again you can order it in small quantities. Now you can provide value to people all over the world. A good CD or DVD kit can sell for £29 – £129 depending on the content.

4 YOU NEED TO 'GOOGLE WELL'

Provided your name isn't Brad Pitt this isn't as challenging as you think either (and even if it is, it's not completely impossible). If you take 2 days of focused effort you can set up a great Facebook club, Ecademy Group, YouTube Channel and an online Forum. You can have a social-network profile on a dozen sites, a twitter account with 400+ followers and a dynamic blog. With all that in place you are going to sky-rocket up the Google listings. Staying there will require you to be diligent but if you are organised, that can take less than 15 mins a day (and it could be done from your iPhone in the back of a cab).

5 YOU NEED TO DO JOINT VENTURES

This final Key is where the money is. You find someone who has a database of contacts who wants to promote you and your products. You find people with complimentary products who can package in with yours. You find a person who has 23,564 twitter followers who can send out a tweet about you. It's through the power of Joint Ventures that your income and your opportunities will explode.

Now you have these five things in place, sit back and watch what happens to your life. People will ask you to speak at events, you will be referred to as an 'expert' or 'well connected' and you will get focused opportunities coming your way.

NEXT STEPS

Daniel Priestley is the Author of "Key Person of Influence - How to become one of the most visible, connected, credible and valuable people in your industry in 6 months". You can also read Daniel's blog:

www.DanielPriestley.com

www.twitter.com/DanielPriestley

PETER
THOMSON

Peter Thomson, known as *The Most Prolific Product Creator* is now regarded as one of the UK's leading strategists on business and personal growth. Starting in business in 1972 he built 3 successful companies – selling the last to a public company, after only 5 years trading, for £4.2M enabling him to retire at age 42.

Since that time Peter has concentrated on sharing his proven methods for business and personal success via audio and video programmes, books, seminars and conference speeches. With over 100 audio and 100 video programmes written and recorded he is Nightingale Conant's leading UK author. Apart from writing and recording programmes, Peter spends part of his time delivering seminars and conference speeches around the world.

Peter is the publisher, writer and presenter of the widely acclaimed audio newsletter www.theachieversedge.com which has sold over 300,000 copies since January 1998.

HOW TO WRITE, CREATE AND MARKET YOUR OWN INFORMATION PRODUCTS

I am thrilled that Peter Thomson, who I consider to be the Godfather of Personal Development in the UK, agreed to be in this book.... but what can I say about him?

Peter was in fact one of the first Mentors I ever had in Business. At the tender age of 25 I studied his material and he had a huge influence on setting my feet on the path to being an Entrepreneur.

In recent years it has been my privilege to work with him one on one - a really fun and rewarding experience I can tell you. Some of The Business Wealth Club Mentors, my office team and even my Wife have been on his courses and used his material in recent years and had real shifts in their perception of Business. We also got great feedback from our Members when we gave them Peter's Secrets of Communication as one of their Books of the Month last year.

Peter's vast body of Products speak for themselves - Thank You Peter for helping to elevate and inspire Business Owners everywhere!

— *Paul Avins*

> It must seem strange to most of the world's business population to even consider the idea of writing then recording then taking the time, expertise and money to market – one's very own informational product.

AND YET...

In this digital age, this high info demanding time, this 'let me tell' you world – it's really no wonder that savvy business owners, in every field, have jumped firmly onto the printing press and joined the ranks of Shakespeare, Bacon and Christie.

The appetite for the written word has increased not diminished as some doom-mongers and naysayers uttered when the 'www' became the de facto way for so many to gain the knowledge they sought and the information they needed.

More people are reading more with the advent of ereaders, Kindles and ipads – multifunctional phones with apps for nigh on every occasion including reading on the train, in bed even whilst walking around. Kindle for iphone, Stanza for Androids, ereader for almost anywhere, anyplace, anytime.

AND DO YOU...

And do I want to get left behind in this wordsmith revolution? Oh no! Why – simply because there are so many, many, many good reasons why we must join.

In the course of just the next few of the first of our minutes together – let me share with you the results of my involvement in the information creation and marketing industry over the last 20 years. Let me during this conversation explain just how – and how easy it is to become a published author, a known voice emanating from the dashboard of your clients' cars. A face shining out from the screen of their PC, Mac or handheld device!

HERE WE GO – HANG ON TIGHT

Let's start as all good journeys start with a three-letter question. You know it, of course, use it everyday, marvelled at its effect as a child. The word and question from one of Kiplings 'honest serving men' is: WHY?

As many a personal development guru would declare: "Once you have a strong enough 'why' the 'how' and 'what' will soon appear" True in my experience.

So – 'why' would you dream of writing, creating and marketing an informational product containing your ideas?

Well – there are a number of key reasons. Let's examine them together.

JUST LOOK...

At almost any field of endeavour and you'll see those at the top (apart from their exploits to get and stay there) are also published authors. Richard Branson, Sir John Harvey Jones when he graced these lands, footballers, TV personalities, singers, chefs and cooks galore. Actors, players of almost anything and Politicians of course.

Let's get clear: Writing a book, creating an audio programme, filming a DVD and any of the myriad derivatives – will give you:

1. Positioning

2. Credibility

3. Power

4. Recognition

5. Authority

My book Business SOS has been one of the best marketing pieces I have ever created

Not to mention, though I'm about to: income – sometimes for life and beyond. Just think of one of the UK's most prolific information product creators. His writings are read across the world, mandatory reading in many schools, and listened to by millions – every year. Did Will imagine it so when he penned so many words back in Stratford upon Avon so long, long ago in the 16th century. I doubt it!

So what a road you may start, a thread pulled from the very fabric of time – oooh.

AND SO...

You go into a meeting with an important potential client. You pass over your pre-prepared agenda, ask for clarification and confirmation of the points you detailed on it then pause a moment whilst your client scans the one page document, finally looks up and confirms their agreement of the document's contents.

Then – before the meeting proper gets underway. You lean forward and with a slight smile offer your 'hoped-to-be' new client a signed copy of your latest book. He takes it, looks at the clever eye-catching design on the front, flips it over to scan your blurbed bio on the reverse and gently opens the book to the first page. You notice his slight disappointment at the fact the book isn't signed – but being a student of people and language you wait. He now in turn leans towards you and asks politely if you'd mind signing this copy for him. You oblige – naturally. And in the moment your 'potential' has become a 'certainty' Relax. I've had it happen, many times.

HOWEVER...

I've also seen the reverse. A new member of staff in an established client – on receiving my offered copy of my latest book, looks somewhat disdainfully at it and then (Horror of Horrors) place his coffee cup on it! I left soon thereafter knowing the connection was severed.

As the old expression so aptly states:

> *"When the first leaf falls we know that autumn has come to the world"*

THE CONTACT CONUNDRUM

So many people say they have a contact list – but when I ask them how often they're in touch with these people – they respond "Not too often". Then I say "Oh so you have a non-contact list rather than a contact list – true?"

One of the easiest ways to maintain contact is to have a Blog, an Ezine or perhaps even better a newsletter. My own newsletter is a Subscription based programme at only £9.97 a month. And yet – over the twelve and a half years it's been published (even at only £9.97 per month) it's generated over £3 million front end income!

Now that's what I call a Compound Effect!

Now you can see why I suggest anyone in business creates and markets their very own information product.

And what better than the occasional (or regular) unsolicited letter extolling your virtues and complimenting you on the efficacy of your ideas and explaining the true difference you've made to someone else's life.

AND NOW...

My final point: All wealth creators know it's highly unlikely that anyone will become wealthy by ONLY swapping their time for money. It's true. You'll run out of the one (time) before you get enough of the other (the money).

So having a stream of secondary passive income from the sales of your books DVDs or CDs – surely has to be worth considering in your strategies or personal and business success.

NEXT STEPS

If you'd like to know precisely how you can easily write, create and market your very own informational product so you can make more money, more easily, more often and still have time to play, then either mouse over to:

www.peterthomson.com

Or call me and explain what you want to achieve:

on 0044 (0) 1926 339901

EXPERT POSITIONING

DANIEL
WAGNER

Daniel Wagner is one the UK's best loved Internet Marketing Mentors. Since his humble beginnings in 2006 - where he made his first dollar online selling dog training ebooks - the Austrian has coached, mentored and inspired thousands worldwide to explore the benefits of internet marketing.

He calls marketing his 'magnificent obsession' and his passion and excitement for the topic shines through every aspect of his business and communication. He strongly believes that marketing and especially using a combination of on and offline marketing are the key to future proof your business for the uncertain times ahead.

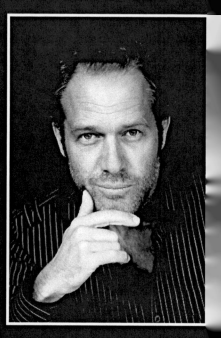

He has generated over $1,000,000 of mainly automated passive income for his companies and his entertaining teaching and mentoring style has made him a frequent presenter on the international stage. His main focus is helping more people understand and leverage the power of the internet to create time and money freedom.

You can learn more about Daniel and how his expertise might be able to help you and your business on www.DanielWagner.com

PACKAGING SECRETS FOR
INFORMATION
PRODUCTS

The first time I saw Daniel on stage he had the audience eating out of his hand! This was quite a few years ago now - and since then we have been lucky enough to welcome him to The Business Wealth Club as an Open Day speaker. Daniel gets great connection with people by speaking in plain, easy to digest language - not jargon (there is a bit of an Austrian twang - but we can forgive him for that!). He really cares about other people's success – and it shows in the results he gets.

— *Paul Avins*

> **In July 2011 I was a silent launch partner and on a single webinar with a JV partner we generated almost $100,000 in just 94 minutes selling an '8 DVD Home Study Course' on mastering Property Auctions.**

My name is Daniel Wagner, I am Austrian (don't hold that against me) and I moved to the UK back in 1995. I was broke for most of my life and dreamed of a career in music. Studying online marketing and making money online has totally transformed my life. I now work as a Marketing Mentor and Success Coach and I love sharing the 'secrets' of my success with my clients and students.

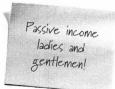

Passive income ladies and gentlemen!

I made my first $5,000 online in 2006 selling dog training ebooks - a market I knew nothing about - as an affiliate and I was so blown away by the easy money that I started teaching how I achieved that. The courses and training programs I developed made me a sought after trainer and speaker on the international stage. I was also able to help thousands of people getting started online and make money for themselves and their businesses.

At the beginning of this year though I had a niggling thought. Could I still 'do it' today? Could I launch a product in a non Internet Marketing niche in this economic climate and make money? Or was I just a Coach or Teacher because I couldn't succeed in the real world?

This case study shares the key components I used and applied to generate almost $100,000 in revenue - many of them transferrable to your business!

I have broken it down into five simple steps. Let me just give you the steps and then put some meat on the bones to flesh out some more detail you can use and/or copy and adjust to your own business or circumstances.

SO HERE ARE THE FIVE SIMPLE STEPS:

1. Choose One of the 4 Evergreen Markets

2. Pick the Ideal 'Expert' Partner

3. Identify the Prospects' 'Hot Buttons'

4. Easily Leverage Reciprocity

5. Apply Advanced Conversion Strategies

Marketing and selling information products is one of the most incredible business models on the planet. Where else do you get to keep 90% of the sale price? There is an endless demand from people eager to learn and discover shortcuts and life changing information!

I want to rush through step 1-4 and focus on step 5 in a bit more detail, as I believe this is where my knowledge and experience can create the biggest difference for you.

1. STAY WITHIN ONE OF THE 4 EVERGREEN MARKETS

In all my years online I have found that there are four key markets that always make money! These are 'deep funnel' markets, meaning customers can potentially stay in them forever and spend large amounts of money to 'improve' their situation.

First up 'Money' - getting out of debts, acquiring it, investing it, growing it, keeping it. With it's submarkets making money online, property investing (real estate for my international readers), stock market investing and business skills.

Second is the massive 'Health' market with losing weight and fitness, looking and feeling better, ridding yourself of disease, (physical, emotional and psychological) and all the supplements of this world!

The third massive market is 'Relationships', from relating to yourself and others to relating to pets (this is huge) and of course finding a partner, keeping a partner or getting rid of a partner!

EXPERT POSITIONING

193

Last up is 'Self Development' and 'Spirituality'. This market is evergreen and includes our search for meaning, metaphysical experiences and answers, from crystals to meditation. At the top of Maslow's hierarchy of needs this is a highly affluent target market.

2. WHEN CHOOSING YOUR 'IDEAL EXPERT', START FROM THE TOP

Go to the best people you can get in touch with and tell them you can add value (not always money) to their lives and businesses. 'How can I help you do more of what you do using what and who I know?' is a great question to start with (fill in specifics please!).

3. TO FIND YOUR PROSPECTS' HOT BUTTONS, USE SURVEYS.

The chosen expert will have access to prospects, so just ask them what they want, then deliver it to them and charge them for it. I use surverymonkey or polldaddy. Tip: keep them short and reward your prospects for taking them.

4. RECIPROCITY IS ONE OF OUR 'INBUILT' AUTOMATIC RESPONSE MECHANISMS.

So the age old 'ask and you'll be given' is replaced by the 'give and you'll be given'. The better the stuff you give away for free the more you'll sell when you offer the opportunity later down the line.

5. ADVANCED CONVERSION STRATEGIES

Let's go into a bit more detail. Here are a few strategies we implemented on our current launch that helped us convert over 35% of prospects on the webinar.

- 'Trial Offer' - we found that the old 'mail order' strategy to pay 'On Approval' massively contributed to our high prospect to sale conversion. While nothing new, it is not done much in the online world which means the opportunity is wide open.

- Our physical 8 DVD set was sent out at £20 and £297 in 30 days with access to a membership site with free updates for a year. There are many ways to create 'trial' offers like this and you have to find your 'sweet spot' between upfront cost and re-bill amount and keep returns in check.

- 'Scarcity'. There are many ways to apply this strategy of influencing your prospects behaviour. Limited amount of places, units, bonuses and of course - only available for a limited time. Make sure you use a deadline! We found that special offer deadlines below 72 hours work best.

- 'Proof'. Use 'social proof', testimonials or case studies of people using your product or service and the results they got from doing so. This will create trust. If you need any inspiration, watch a couple of hours of QVC or some of the Guthy Renker infomercials (the proactiv acne treatment informercial is one of my favourites!).

- 'Packaging Strategies'. How your product arrives at your valued customer is a big part of your sales success. 'Consumption' starts the moment they take delivery. Many of the little 'tricks' are free or very low cost to implement and will dramatically reduce return rates of your product and therefore increase profits.

Good packaging including cellophane wrapping your DVDs and high quality boxes create a great first impression. Better DVD boxes are just a few extra pence! Many times your customer will make a 'value' decision within seconds of seeing your product.

A simple 'lift note', a post it note with a 'call this number now for a special message' note helps to frame the customers' experience before they open the DVDs. I have found freespeech.co.uk an excellent free provider for my free recorded message. I also use speedystamps.co.uk to produce a stamp to look like a hand written message.

We included a three page colour welcome letter and un-announced bonuses on high quality paper in an envelope in the box.

EXPERT POSITIONING

195

My last 'killer tip' is to use the back cover of the DVD wisely. Paul always says 'a book is bought in three stages, first the cover, then the back cover, then when you flick through it'.

Your DVD or CD product is 'evaluated' and bought in just two steps. Cover and back cover. Yet most info products I see have a blank back! What a waste of space that will cost you thousands!

Below is an example of one of our DVD sleeves. Let me point out a few features we found helps our value proposition.

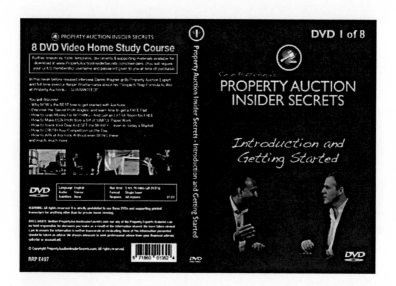

First you can see it is part of a set. If it should ever find it's way to another prospect, it's clear there is more. People have a need to complete a set and collect. It's in our nature.

Second we tell them there is lots more content online in the members' area. This assures that 'copycats' will not get the full benefit of the customer. It also allows for easy updates. My Tip: put strategic and fundamentals on the DVD, instructions, tactics and updates online. Aim for a shelf life of three years!

The obvious stuff is putting customer benefits and content bullets on the back of the DVD. Start your bullets with 'How to' and an action verb and you're in safe territory! A variety of images – from different locations to create trust – are also common.

But there are some less used little gems we always use, that will increase the perceived value and create trust through familiarity:

the DVD logo (in at least three places), a bar code (even if the DVD will never reach the shelves of HMV), a RRP (Recommended Retail Price = suggested value), the DVD region code, audio and subtitle details and running time, a disclaimer and copyright.

A killer tip on the copyright: Leave off the year as you avoid having your product appear dated next year!

And never call your product: 'The top tips for [insert year]!' You will regret it – I promise.

The point I am making is that people will look at the back and un-consciously make a split second decision if this is a 'professional' product. What is their reference and comparison? Check out any of your Hollywood collection for inspiration. Be smart, copy!

One of my favourite strategies – Swipe and Deploy!

Do whatever you can to enhance your customers experience. If you ever bought a polo shirt at Hugo Boss or any other designer label, you'll know exactly what I mean about 'packaging strategy'. It's no different here.

Your product is bought with a promise and delivered in its packaging. So your packaging holds the promise! Always remember that.

Product launches, marketing and selling information products are an easy and profitable addition to any business. Marketing and understanding psychology are amongst the most powerful skills to study and master and they will - used well - directly impact your bottom line profits.

NEXT STEPS

If you want to find out more about my work and passion, just hop over to:

www.DanielWagner.com *to learn more.*

CASH MAY BE KING BUT MAKING MONEY AND KEEPING THE MONEY YOU MAKE ARE TWO DIFFERENT SKILLS. START LEARNING THESE CRITICAL SKILLS FOR WEALTH CREATION TODAY...

MON

& MA

EY
RGIN

MARIE-CLAIRE CARLYLE

Marie-Claire Carlyle has spent most of her working life coaching people to achieve 6 figure incomes, both in the corporate world and as owner of her own company, working principally with entrepreneurs. Creator of the original one day *Money Magnet Workshop* and author of the book *How to become a Money Magnet!* (Hay House Publishing), Marie-Claire holds two business degrees and she balances business principles and proven sales techniques with the world of energy and quantum physics, to deliver consistent results.

Marie-Claire herself, went from being quite possibly the worst ever salesperson in Xerox to achieving over £1 million sales every month as Sales Director of a software company and is passionate about empowering you to realise your full value, in every sense of the word. Increasingly popular as a truly inspirational speaker, she is currently writing her next book, *Money Magnet Miracles*.

HOW TO BECOME A
MONEY
MAGNET

I defy anyone not to be drawn to Marie-Claire's energy! You know how some people just have it... well she does!

I was first on stage with her at a Wealth Wizard Seminar - and I was so inspired by her message that I couldn't wait to give her book "How to become a Money Magnet" to our Wealth Club Members as a Book of the Month. They loved it and I know you will too!

— *Paul Avins*

> Why is it that one actor can be an overnight success whilst another treads the boards of obscurity all their life? How is it that one business owner can work night and day just to make ends meet, when another strikes it lucky with whatever he touches?

It can't just be down to straightforward hard work. I know plenty of hard working people who are struggling to make ends meet, don't you?

It can't be down to knowledge alone. I know plenty of clever people who have hordes of teams to support them and yet are struggling to pay the school fees.

> **The key differentiator between someone who is fortunate and someone who isn't is in their mindset.**

This is not just positive thinking. Positive thinking on top of negative beliefs won't kid anyone, least of all your bank manager! Doing affirmations are great but they won't change your bank account. Worse than that, affirming that you have all the money you need when you know that you can't afford the next phone bill is called lying to yourself. The only person that you are kidding is yourself.

> **So the first thing you need to do is to get really straight with yourself. Look at your business with an objective eye. How much money is in your bank account? If it's less than you would expect or want, there is something missing in how you are around your business.**

Are you being resigned? Are you being a victim to what's happening with the economy or with the banks? Have you given up believing in your staff? Have you given up trusting yourself?

There is a key principle called the 'Be Do Have Principle'. Most of us get it wrong. We think that when we have the £1 million in the bank we can then do all the things we want to do and we can then be happy. So we live in a perpetual state of "life will be better when....". It is an exhausting way to live. It causes stress and has an impact on the people we love. And it keeps the money that you aspire to attract in the future!

When you change the way you are being around money you will start to do things differently and then you will attract the money you desire. For example, one of my clients established that she was being scared of money. What she was doing was putting all her bills unopened on the sideboard. Not knowing how much she had to pay left her with a fear that she wouldn't have enough, and she became increasingly fearful of money. In this state, not surprisingly, money eluded her, irrespective of what she did.

Great Wealth Tip!

When she declared that she was now being "powerful and creative" with money, she started to open her bills the moment they arrived. She told me how she became excited about finding ways to pay her bills promptly! In this new state of mind she went on to ask for a pay rise at work and she agreed an extra bonus with her boss. What would you do differently if you were being powerful and creative around money?

Another client called me because he had identified a significant and regular leakage in his personal finances. No matter how hard he worked, things just seemed to keep happening that robbed him of his money. We took a look into how he was being with money and how he had been in the past with money. What came up was that years ago he had done a property deal that had gone wrong. He'd ended up leaving potential investors empty handed and without their deposits. In other words, he had robbed them of their money. On some level, albeit unconscious, his guilt at what had happened was in the way of him being able to attract and keep his money. By resolving to be honest and open with money he then took the action to contact the investors and offer to repay them in full. After that the money started to flow in.

MONEY & MARGINS

> The first step in becoming a Money Magnet is to TAKE RESPONSIBILITY for what is showing up in your life; to acknowledge that there is something in how you are being towards money that is having a direct impact on the amount of money you are attracting

Be straight about how much money you have (that means being on top of your accounts) and how much money you want. Give up any 'story' about why you don't have enough. It's not the fault of your customers, the banks, the economy or even the politicians. What is it that you are not doing?

> If you don't have enough clients, what is it that you are not doing that you could do? And WHY aren't you doing it? Or what is the benefit of NOT doing it?

Susan was complaining that her business wasn't very successful. We established that she had an issue with earning lots of money. She didn't like the imbalance between the wealthy and the impoverished in the world. So the benefit to her of not being successful was that she got to think of herself as a good person. That is a powerful incentive to hold back on being too successful. It wasn't until she could see that her "pretending" not to be who she really was was not going to help anyone, least of all those who were aspiring to achieve what she was achieving. In diminishing her own greatness she was also in danger of making her customers wrong for choosing to do business with her! Not a good strategy for a successful business!

Are you playing full out and taking massive action in your business? *Are you 100% committed to your financial goals?* The FAB principle refers to Focus Action and Belief. Action without focus is just keeping busy. Action without Belief in the desired outcome is a commitment to failure.

You need to take action.....but action without a Money Magnet mindset will have a limited impact.

Massive Action
=
Massive Results

NEXT STEPS

Register for your FREE ten day online course in How to become a Money Magnet at:

www.marieclairecarlyle.com

MONEY & MARGINS

DAVE
HOLLAND

David started his career as a Weapons Engineer within Royal Ordnance and progressed through a variety of industries as diverse as Packaging and Logistics, Dance Sport, Aviation and Recruitment Services.

He has worked as a Manager, Director and Business Owner, his most recent role, prior to founding Results RULES OK was that of CEO EMEA for a Global Organisation based out of Luxembourg; having previously spent 2 years as Director of Training based out of USA. Having worked and presented in 20 Countries, with an MBA and a passion for business and people, David continues to build Results RULES OK into an increasingly international organization delivering world class programs, events and resources to a diverse range of people, enabling everyone to enjoy learning, achieving, doing and being more...

David is now an Author, Speaker, Trainer and Advisor to business owners, entrepreneurs and everyone with an interest in business success.

CONTRADICTION BY
NUMBERS

I have called Dave (Dutch) Holland a friend since we both cut our Business Coaching teeth in Action Coach in 2003. Since then we shared stages, bars and laughs all around the World, and I was very chuffed when he was able to find the time to write this chapter. In my early days - numbers were my achilles heel.

Dutch was the man who helped me to not only understand them - but to enjoy and get excited about them. So when I needed a kick ass finance workshop for the members of The Business Wealth Club - Dutch was the Mentor I called. By the way.... he's a mean drummer as well!

— *Paul Avins*

> The language of business is numbers, a business can look good, feel good and even taste good; but unless the numbers are right – you won't have a business, you'll just have a very expensive hobby...

My challenge and opportunity therefore is to make your business numbers as compelling and exciting as the passion you have for every other aspect of your life; so here goes...

Contrary thinking is simply finding a way of asking better questions, thinking differently – and not being afraid to be the dissenting voice. I remember attending a board meeting as a young Operations Manager; the Directors were contemplating strategic choices and investment plans for the coming year. I had been invited there to give a "real world" opinion on their ideas.

I was given three scenarios that they wanted me to consider;

1. *Buying key competitors.*

2. *Aggressive Sales & Marketing.*

3. *Buying key players in the supply chain.*

I was asked to rank them in order of preference, and was asked by the Chairman if I had any questions. I did...

I looked up and asked – "why do we need to grow..?"

The Chairman, looked at me with a cold stare – he was either going to fire me for stupidity or promote me for impudence. Here's what happened...

He asked each Director in turn exactly why they believed that the business had to grow in order to be more successful in the future. One after another they stammered out the stock phrases like "critical mass", "leverage", "brand", "economies of scale", "market leadership" and even "penetration through diversification of portfolio" – I remember the last one particularly well.

I was thanked and asked to leave the room...

Some weeks later, I had a telephone call from the Chairman, asking to see me. As I entered his office he simply reached into his desk drawer and took out his car keys.

"Here" he said as he tossed them to me – "I want you to go home now, take your wife out to lunch and convince her that moving to Bristol to run one of my companies there is a good idea.."

"I will see you when you get back here by 17.00hrs..."

Simply put, we didn't need to grow; we needed to get better at what we already did – then we could grow...

So here are my top *7 Business Number Contradictions* that will help you become truly successful...

CONTRADICTION 1: PROFIT IS NOT YOUR OBJECTIVE

Got to love a 7 Step Checklist!

Your objective is to build your business to achieve what you want. Once you are clear on exactly why you are in business, we can make a plan. Now while of course you need to make a profit in your business, profit is simply a barometer that lets you know how you are doing, your focus and attention should be on the causes of profit – your objective is to understand what causes profit in your business and manage them so that you can achieve your why.

> **Profit is your Objective when you know why, and how to generate it...**

CONTRADICTION 2:
CASH IS NOT KING

Cash will produce approximately nothing while it is sat in your account, it will make you feel good and able to sleep at night, but that is all. Cash should be invested in assets and resources that give you a return. *For example, the only reason you should pay a wage is because you get a better return on the investment than leaving it in the bank or trading on the markets.* It is how you invest your cash that is King, not how you store it. When your cash actually works for you, you will make sure you collect all that is due on time, every time – it will be really expensive when you don't...

> **Cash is King when it is invested well...**

CONTRADICTION 3:
GROWTH IS NOT GOOD.

Plenty of profitable businesses close down because they simply grow too fast, they cannot keep pace with the investment required. Imagine a business with revenues of £5 million in 2009 that grows steadily so it achieves total revenue of £6 million in 2010. That's just a 20% increase; but if in January 2010 the sales were around £420k (about 1/12 of the £5 million), to achieve £6 million during the year, assuming steady growth, the sales in December 2010 would need to be around £600k – compared to January that is a change of 42%, not 20% and even if growth stops there – the business will have a running rate of £600k per month, or £7.2 million a year – growing a massive 71%.. Understanding the implications of growth is fundamental to your success – 20% growth = 71% bigger...

> **Growth is good, only when it is managed and understood...**

CONTRADICTION 4:
BIG CONTRACTS ARE BAD

I have a rule that in any of my companies, one client should represent no more than 10% of my profits. Winning a big contract looks very attractive, especially when you are going for growth – they can be the worst thing that happens to a business. Watch out for tight margins, extended payment terms, and queries raised on your invoices from eager employees' in their Purchase ledger department. If you do go for a big contract, make sure you keep marketing to find others that will dilute their control over you – don't allow a customer to have more control over your business than your shareholders...

> **Big Contracts are great when they contribute to your business not overwhelm it...**

CONTRADICTION 5:
AVOID DISCOUNTING.

Never ever discount your prices – and don't be fooled by Manufacturers Recommended Retail Prices either... If you make 50% gross profit on an item, and you offer a discount of 25% you will instantly cut your profits in half on every sale. This means that in order to get a benefit from the offer you have got to sell more than twice the amount you would have done at the full price – sounds like working harder to stand still to me... If you put your prices up by 10% on the same item – you could afford to sell fewer and still make the same profit – there are always choices when it comes to pricing, and maintaining your margins is the art of a successful business.

> **Pricing is the essence of your success – protect your margins wherever possible...**

MONEY & MARGINS

CONTRADICTION 6:
OVERHEADS ARE GOOD

Very few people build a great business by simply cutting costs. Your overheads are usually made up of the salaries and wages of your team, premises costs and other operational necessities. They are not overheads when they all give you a positive return on your investment – see Contradiction 2. When every team member gives you a positive return, you can hire as many as you like, when you pay rent for a great location that generates business for you, open more branches in similar locations.

Every line of overhead should be viewed as an investment from which you need to get a return – your insurance broker should pass you referrals, so should your bank and telephone provider. When every overhead is truly working for your business – overheads are indeed good.

> **Overheads are bad – only when they are out of control...**

CONTRADICTION 7:
ACCOUNTS ARE BORING

I love looking at my accounts – now you may say that I need to get out more, but once we understand our business, we can actually start to enjoy looking at how our business is doing. Your accounts should be regular, monthly for the full management accounts but have daily and weekly numbers prepared that will show you what is happening. Select a range of indicators that will let you know how everything and everyone is performing. Marketing, service and operations should all have measures and performance targets to achieve – that will mean when you look at the accounts you will be pleasantly surprised and not unduly shocked.

Accounts are exciting when they tell you good news...

NEXT STEPS

A full set of supporting templates and documents is available at:

www.resultsrulesok.com

If you have got this far, then we should probably discuss how I can help you and your business achieve extraordinary results. Whether it is coming along to one of our events, arranging a keynote presentation or working with me on a 1:1 basis – let's explore the possibilities...

Contact me today at my personal email address davidholland@resultsrulesok.com to find out more – and relax; I don't bite and I don't charge anyone for finding out more..

SOHAIL
KHAN

Sohail Khan has over 15 years of sales and joint venture marketing and business experience.

Having previously built a multi-million pound internet training business which he started with just £1000 in 2000 - he then sold a majority stake to a £75M IT Company in 2006. After just 2 years the IT Company went bust - and Sohail lost everything, except of course his expertise for building a business with over £3.5 Million in sales using just joint ventures.

So, picking himself up - Sohail set himself a challenge to make over £1m within 12 months using nothing but joint ventures. Without a product, business or capital Sohail identified his first "biggest" joint venture to date (within 30 days). A company that had over 4 million customers and in this one connection is set to make over £1M in it's first year - with a further £3M in year 3... this real life strategy is now the basis for Sohails "Joint Venture Blueprint!"

His results got him noticed by some of the biggest names in online and off-line marketing, and he has joint ventured with them to create The JV University and the International Joint Venture Consulting Certification.

HOW TO CONNECT WITH MILLIONAIRES AND BILLIONAIRES

> Sohail and I first met over 5 years ago at a seminar I was giving local business owners on how to improve their Sales and Marketing.
>
> We stayed in contact via e-mails over the years until we both met up again on the Speaking Circuit, he was speaking on JV's - I was speaking on Turbo Charging your Profits. As this is such a Key topic in the new economy I invited him to speak at my Oxford Business Wealth Club and members still reference his training session today. For BIG thinking JV Strategy that can add Millions to your business he is the best there is in my view, judge for yourself.
>
> — *Paul Avins*

Most people know me as the Joint Venture Expert and 'Master Connector' as I have the ability to connect with almost anybody including Millionaires and Billionaires. One thing I have learnt from making millions, losing them and then becoming a millionaire again very quickly is that it is all about the people I surround myself with and that has helped accelerate my wealth!

There is a famous quote by Robert Kiyosaki that comes to mind:

> **"If you managed to be in millionaire environments every second of your life, wouldn't it make sense that you'll stay a millionaire or become a millionaire one day?"**

Great question!

You have heard the saying 'the 5 people in your network determines your net worth' right? Your network is simply a community that you are in. This community has rules, values and beliefs of its own that eventually become your values and beliefs. You have to be extremely selective in choosing your network. Remember that millionaires network with millionaires. To identify if you are in the right network, identify the topics of your conversations when you are in your community. Do you talk about creating wealth, being a better husband or wife or simply the weather?

Most times these Millionaires are the Core Influences in any given industry because of their wealth and financial business success. If you want to become the best in your business field you must take the initiative of connecting with the Core Influencers, you must cultivate their endorsements. Encourage them to respond to your offering in a positive way by connecting using some of my own techniques which I will cover. I will show you how to connect... By doing so, you too can also become a success in a small fraction of the time that is often required otherwise.

Research has shown that millionaires turn networks into chequebooks — they leverage who and what they already know. They get information, introductions, advice, financial support, emotional support and practical support.

CONNECT WITH MILLIONAIRES AND BILLIONAIRES

I get more as I give because I actively listen to the other person, to their needs. This is easier said than done. Here is an example, see if you can help them address their needs; don't be afraid to ask "How can I be helpful?" or "Would it be helpful if I ..." Maybe they need an intro to a firm or a person — I call this "connecting the dots" — and if you do that, you become more "relevant" to that person. And they'll be there for you, too. So don't focus on what you can get, that will come naturally if you give.

In the past it was much harder to connect with Millionaires and Billionaires however, now there is no reason why you can't get to people you don't know, thanks to the Social Media tools online today like Facebook and LinkedIn. Social Media is now used by everyone including millionaires to billionaires so you now don't even have to fight the gatekeepers to get hold of them. These Social Media tools allow you to manage your contacts more effectively, and you can manage the information that you get from these people.

I use Social Media a lot to find the 'Core Influencers' and always commend them on something that they have done recently or I mention a paragraph from their book that I'm reading. What happens is that they usually get back with a thank you and now the dialogue can begin as I slowly bring them onto a call to ask them about their projects and how I can help them sell more of their product or service. My whole ethos is centred around, 'Give First, Ask Later' and guess what, it works! Always remember it's not about you, making that honest connection and giving value is the key!

Also, even when rejected, there's always something positive you can get out of it. So go into a meeting or an encounter prioritizing your goals and if you're rejected, consider how else you can create a "win" — maybe they become an advisor or mentor to you? Maybe they make an introduction for you?

High level connectors like me gain endorsements for reasons that go beyond the basic product or service I offer. We do extraordinary things, that is the difference. For example, I always enhance the profit/sales of whoever I'm connecting with first. In other words I always open with the question, 'How Can I Help You Sell More Of Your Product or Service?' I will always give this help before asking them for anything and in return the Millionaire will then go out of his way to endorse me to his network.

Most millionaires and billionaires that I know are members of one or more affinity groups. These groups include professional societies, philanthropotic associations, political groups, alumni associations and even masterminds (as mentioned in Napolean Hill's Think and Grow Rich).

I myself just got back recently from spending a few days with some of the top millionaires and billionaires in America. I was at a billionaire's 40,000 sq foot mansion in Tampa. I don't know about you, but I have never been in such a big house!

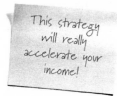

This strategy will really accelerate your income!

I recently had the opportunity to be invited to and join a $25,000 Mastermind group run by a friend of Tony Robbins. Let me tell you something, after just one meeting I felt as if I had been catapulted to an entirely new level! Why? Because I was surrounded with incredibly bright, talented, successful and generous millionaires and billionaires who were just as interested in my success as I am in theirs. What an incredible feeling!

To connect with millionaires and billionaires YOU must provide something of value to them. Don't forget these are extremely busy people and do not have time for idle chit chat! I believe everybody has something to offer and the important need here is a solution to remove their pain or problems. If you dedicate yourself to serve others then you will make that CONNECTION.

Also, develop yourself as a leader and winner, as success only breeds success. Be interesting and have a really cool story that you can share, make them want to connect with you! I have made so many 'high-level' connections because of this strategy.

Remember , you attract the people you think about. The Law of attraction really does work if you think about attracting prosperity and millionaires into your life and you take action towards those things, you are increasing the chance that it will happen; or something even better!

I challenge you to think about the people you are networking with and are surrounded by. Are they where you want to go? Or, are they where you are? Do they support you? Or, are they secretly threatened by your success? I think it's important to be in a variety of 'high-level' networking groups.

THERE ARE THREE CATEGORIES:

Those groups that allow you to really give to the other members or those you serve

Those groups that include your peers

Those groups that will really stretch you!

The third group is KEY because it will give you a chance to grow and stretch to the next level so you can truly reach your highest and greatest potential!

NEXT STEPS

Evaluate the networking groups you are involved with today. Are they balanced like the example above?

If not, are you ready and willing to make a change? By when?

If you are interested in learning more about how I went from 'Zero to 4 Million Customers In Just 30 Days' and how I use the power of Joint Ventures and Social Media to connect with the top 'Core Influencers' in any given Industry get a copy of my FREE DVD at:

www.freejointventuredvd.com

Or to find out more about my JC Club go to:

www.theJVClub.com

JEFF
LERMER

At 6 Jeff decided he wanted to be an accountant, whilst other children wanted to be football players and train drivers. He loved numbers, always felt comfortable with them and thought his Dad's accountant was glamorous. Well he had a great car and smoked cigars, all very enticing for a 6 year old!

By 38 he found himself sitting on the fence. Happy and comfortable working for a Firm in partnership, earning a good income, but felt he could do much better for clients, and felt restricted in partnership format, so he left and set up on his own.

Through hard work and continued learning, both personal and professional development, his practice grew and today his Practice employs 13 people, six qualified accountants, 4 qualified by experience and three administrators.

In 2006 he joined the tax committee of the Association of Chartered Certified Accountants and in 2008 and 2009 he was one of the speakers at the ACCA budget breakfast.

He has just completed his first book, *Lights, Camera, Accountancy – How to Pay Less Tax in the Entertainment Industry.*

KEEPING HOLD OF THE MONEY YOU MAKE

If you want to build serious Wealth you'll need a great Accountant in your Power Team of advisors. We have many great accountants in the Business Wealth Clubs who fit this description but I wanted to introduce you to a man who proves why all Accountants are not created equal, and how to identify the right one for you.

Jeff and I first met at a one day Workshop I was running and I went on to Coach him and his team. As I got to see and experience his knowledge and skill in advanced Tax Strategies and Wealth protection planning, I asked him to work with me and a number of my high end Coaching Clients. His advice has helped many of them legally make and keep hundreds of thousands of pounds in additional Profits and Personal income and proves the point that it's not how much you make, but how much you keep that counts!

His chapter will help you see if it's time to change Your Accountant to one with greater Wealth awareness!

— *Paul Avins*

> With over 20 years experience as a Chartered Accountant and specialist Tax Advisor, looking after the affairs of over 400 organisations & 650 individuals, you would think that there wouldn't be many things left in the exciting world of accountancy that would actually shock me.

However, in my profession, one thing which is virtually guaranteed to shock me is the extent to which almost every new or potential client we meet possesses little or no formal tax strategy, whether they be covering short, medium or long term aspirations. The regularity of this is actually quite alarming.

But how can this be the case? When you consider that most Accountants websites look the same; boasting, amongst other things, a proactive service and offering tax planning & strategies – but it would regrettably appear that very few actually deliver on these promises.

For this reason, I do have some degree of sympathy for clients when they have to appoint a new accountant because, in reality, they are not fully armed with all the information necessary to be able to make what is an important decision: Is this the right firm for me, my circumstances and my aspirations?

How true!

Of course, there are some fantastic accountants & tax advisors out there, but it can be very difficult for clients to differentiate between good and bad, or even to identify a good one when they already act for you. Often the decision is made on a more superfluous level – convenience, personality & presentation. But making the right decision needs to be based on having access to the right information, and asking the right questions.

Let us look at a simple example. If I were to ask you if your savings were in bank accounts that offered you the best rate of return, I suspect that most would say it was about right. One contributing reason is the wealth of information that investors have at their fingertips regarding savings accounts – the internet & media in general are awash with easily accessible data on rates of interest, terms & conditions, special offers etc. for these products. Ultimately you can be absolutely certain that your money is in the best possible account if you spend just the shortest amount of time checking the public domain.

If we compare this transparency to you running your business & the role any potential advisor may play in supporting you, how would you know whether every tax break and angle is looked at, every available expense claimed or even whether you are trading as the most effective entity – be it sole trader, partnership, limited liability partnership (LLP) or limited company. I suspect that, in truth, you would have little or no idea. At this point, ensuring you have the right Accountant can actually make a real difference.

> **One useful exercise we do when we take on new clients is to prepare a strategic roadmap, wherein we identify & attempt to fully understand a persons goals, plans & aspirations, and also their own specific living requirements. If a couple can live on £6,000 per month net of tax, why operate an inefficient remuneration structure that generates £10,000 per month?**

For example, one client I recently took on had, what they perceived to be, a sensible remuneration package. The husband was on a £30,000 per annum salary, and his wife received £20,000. On top of this, the husband also drew £70,000 in dividends.

MONEY & MARGINS

By talking through their aims & goals, and understanding both their family circumstances & matters specific to how they live, it soon became apparent that the remuneration could be adjusted. By changing the salary structure, dividends and expenses we increased the net family income by £25,000 per annum – without costing the company anything at all!

This is just one example amongst many, where the right advice can help you & your business save money. The purpose of this chapter, however, is not to say "we know best", because that isn't necessary. Instead, it's primary aim is to highlight the importance of setting short, medium & long term goals. And how understanding & acting towards these goals can actively help you to keep more of the money you make!

SHORT TERM GOALS

If you are a limited company, there are different aspects that could help you to save money. These are:

PARENTS OR CHILDREN

It is not uncommon for parents or children to get involved in the running of a family business. It can often be all hands to the deck.

When family members are involved in the business, and own equity in the company, they are entitled to receive dividends. As long as the children are over 18 years of age, they would be taxed in their own right. Remember though, that any funds paid must be remitted to the respective bank accounts of the children or parents.

VEHICLE

Vehicles are an important element of any business. Your advisor should be able to look at which vehicle you use for work & private use, and ensure that, where possible, the maximum tax advantages are taken care of.

VAT SCHEMES

There are a number of VAT Schemes that could be operated for the company, and it can often make a surprising amount of difference if you operate within the wrong scheme. The flat rate scheme, for example, for smaller turnover businesses (less than £150k pa), allows you to charge VAT at the full amount, yet pay a lower percentage of the vat-able amount to the Inland Revenue. It is not uncommon for certain clients to save up to £3,000 per year in Value Added Tax, in addition to any indirect savings resulting from the reduced administrative burden of maintaining a much simpler scheme.

EXPENSES

You need to consider specific expenses that incur for the business, and check that they are properly claimed for.

INCOME OF THE OWNER

There is no need to pay an owner of a Limited company a large PAYE salary. If they are not a director, then they must be paid at least the amount equal to the minimum wage, and if they are a director, minimum wage legislation does not come into effect.

In the year to 5 April 2011, an individual can earn just under £44,000 without entering the higher 40% tax bracket. Leading on from this a cost effective remuneration structure may restrict their salary to, say, £5,700 per annum, and accrue for dividends of £34,300. In this way, assuming there exists no other income, there will be no higher rate tax liability. Importantly, so long as a PAYE Scheme is submitted, the individual will still qualify for a State Pension in retirement.

One area subject to much debate, is that of income splitting. More often than not, the owner of a business will have a life partner, and will need to consider whether their partners will have some shares in the business, and if so what type of shares – and thus what rights and benefits they confer - if they are involved in the business. Whilst the Inland Revenue have stated that they are unhappy with income splitting, the Government has effectively shelved any legislation to change the current rules.

MONEY & MARGINS

This is not a complete list of what can be considered, but it does highlight the fact that in the short term the company should attempt to set up a remuneration structure that matches family circumstances.

MEDIUM TERM

Whilst short term goals are often aimed at matching family circumstances, it can be useful to have a "Medium Term" tax strategy. Such a strategy might, for example, target paying off a mortgage, or to properly fund a pension scheme. The goals and aspirations of the business ownership should be considered, and a good tax advisor would be able to assimilate this information and suggest the best method or vehicle to meet these medium term aspirations. For example, a Limited Liability Partnership (LLP) can be especially useful for producing a Capital Gain that can be used to clear a personal mortgage. Any advice in this area, however, needs to be very case specific, so having a clear, detailed and definite plan is essential.

Plan, plan, plan!

LONG TERM ASPIRATIONS

Long term aspirations often involve selling the business. And the type of entity that you trade in will affect the amount of tax payable as a result of any sale.

Commonly, people trade to companies. If you are trading this way, it is desirable, when selling, to sell the shares of the Limited Company. By doing this you will ensure a lower rate of Capital Gains Tax on the sale, however, it may not be particularly helpful from a prospective purchasers point of view. A purchaser, looking to buy the shares in your company, would have to carry out a full due diligence on the companies activities, and if any due diligence revealed, say, an under declaration in VAT some years previously, then the purchaser would be responsible for that liability. Quite often, the complexity and breadth of any due diligence results in the compliance cost for a company sale being significantly higher than for a sale involving goodwill only. Purchasers, when buying shares in Ltd Companies, are unable to offset any tax liability they suffered when they bought the shares.

If, however, a purchaser bought shares in a sole trader business, an LLP, or just purchased a traders goodwill, then any goodwill is available to be offset against their tax liability if they acquired it through a Limited Company. There would be no additional tax payable by you, the vendor, on a company sale – subject to limits and anti-avoidance, and it would also qualify at the lower rate of Capital Gains Tax.

Therefore, when considering any long term strategy involving a disposal of your business, how you trade and whether you trade using an LLP or Ltd Company can have vital consequences within a sale.

Regardless of how you trade, you need to ensure that everything within the business is in good order & the way you run the business is extremely tidy. Proper contracts of employment, good organisation of statutory affairs, formal records of insurances, up to date financial records & affairs are all areas that will allow any accountants carrying out a due diligence exercise, prior to a potential sale, to have as smooth a job as possible. I have personally seen a number of transactions fail at latter stages as a result of matters arising out of due diligence, so the importance of maintaining good order cannot be understated.

NEXT STEPS

To find out more about how we could help you with all of this planning, visit our web site:

www.lermer.co.uk

MONEY & MARGINS

MARCELLUS LINDSAY

Known as The "i2i Coach", Marcellus delivers services that take an individual or organisation from their original idea, through successful implementation on to the point of income generation – avoiding pain, costs and the pitfalls that can occur without his assistance. His approach is based upon three basic stages on the path to profit and flow (The 3 I Framework): Idea, Implementation and Income.

Marcellus is a dynamic Business Coach, Talent Dynamics Practitioner and Consultant with over 25 years management and leadership experience with expertise in turning around failing projects (Prince 2 Certified) for some of the largest companies in the UK.

Business and Community Contribution are equally important to Marcellus. So as well as being the Mentor for the Birmingham Business Wealth Club, he is also Co Founder of The Biz Boot Camp Ltd, a not for profit organisation that mentors and supports young entrepreneurs to start and stay in business while connecting and contributing to social action. He is also founder of Catalysts for Community, an organisation that assists impactful community service organisations that are typically overlooked by large funders.

IMPLEMENTATION OF IDEAS
DRIVES YOUR
INCOME!

It's always nice to share time with an audience after I speak. To chat through peoples Business dreams, hear their concerns and to get their feedback on the ideas and strategies I've shared. Often people want to know how they can get hold of my books, CD's etc, and many people want to find out about how they can visit a Business Wealth Club.

In all the years I have been speaking, I have only ever once been stopped in my tracks by somebody demanding, in fact almost rugby tackling me to the ground, to speak to me about opening a Club with me - that person was Marcellus!

What immediately struck me as we spoke was the clarity of his vision to help his local business community. His commitment to do whatever it would take to become a Mentor and his intense desire to make a difference.

The more I have gotten to know and work with him as he launched his Birmingham Club the more impressed I have been. Trust me when I tell you this is a man on a mission who will not be distracted from his Goal. His energy, enthusiasm and practical approach to building growing businesses are a unique mix. Add to that his knowledge of Wealth Tools like Talent Dynamics, and this is a man you will want on your team!

I am very proud to have him on the BWC team and very glad I decided to travel into London one hot sunny Sunday to speak at the event where we first met.

Make sure you experience him live for yourself and get along to his Birmingham Club - this is a man who helps his Members get things... Done!

— Paul Avins

> *It has been said that "Ideas are the beginning points of all fortunes" Without ideas there would be no industry, commerce or civilisation as we know it.*

So, what separates good ideas from the great ideas... the ones that build a fortune? A simple, yet powerful answer - 'Implementation'.

You can use other words such as 'action', 'dedication' or 'follow through' but the result is the same. An idea must move from the ethereal to something that can be seen, heard, felt and understood by others in order to generate income or a desired benefit.

Although this conclusion is very logical and makes complete sense, it takes some people a lifetime to actually grasp and apply the concept. Knowledge is only Power if you apply it after all.

I want to share with you a strategy that I discovered after working with creative people and organisations for over 25 years, which changed my life and can change yours.

You're about to learn:

- Why ideas are at the heart of human progress, growth and development

- What are some of the key characteristics of a good business idea

- What steps you should take to implement your ideas so they generate income

- Who you should have on your team for generating ideas

- Where to go to get help implementing your ideas

- How to keep the ideas coming – one of the key skills of an Entrepreneur

In this chapter I'll focus on business ideas - whether it's the basis for a new business or an idea to improve and grow an existing business.

This can be applied to your situation whether you are

- In business and searching for the next big thing to add value and grow

- Starting a business with an idea that you believe is the basis for a profitable Company

- In a role and want to use your ideas to demonstrate the value you and they can add to the organisation

A key characteristic that separates the millionaire entrepreneur from the rest of society is how well they were able to implement despite the challenges and obstacles their idea faced. In fact, the concept doesn't even have to be original. The application of the concept may be the "new idea" that improves the way value is delivered or leveraged as global brands like Apple have proved many times.

Applying what you learn in this chapter can be the difference between frustration (business bankruptcy) and fulfilment (business wealth).

For a Business to succeed it Must keep doing two things – Marketing and Innovating the way it does business. The ability to generate a constant fresh stream of ideas to aid these two objectives is essential.

If you are a creative person you tend to operate and thrive in a creative frequency of energy. You may have ideas every week, day or even every hour. When the ideas come flooding in it can sometimes feel almost overwhelming and hard to get them all out into a format that can be used by others.

The danger is over time, the ideas pile up within you, and you begin to undervalue the innovation because of the feeling of overwhelm or the perception of lack of resources, and the constant battle with the "How?" question.

Take a moment to write below the top 5 Reasons or Excuses You use that Stop you Implementing Your Ideas:

1. ....

2. ....

3. ....

4. ....

5. ....

If you can't be 100% honest with yourself you'll never be able to move forward to the success you desire.

All of these reasons or excuses as I like to call them, often lead to the idea staying in your head and heart. Over time, the ideas well up, become stagnant and no longer serve to refresh you, but rather, they may become the source of regret, frustration or bitterness.

But there is hope...

The simple act of reading this book means that you are ready to get back in touch with your passion. You are aware and are ready to ACT. You are equipping yourself with the steps and the strategy that has been proven time and time again to yield results. And results will ensure and motivate you to take another small step.

Remember, as we like to say at the end of every Business Wealth Club Meeting – "You get paid on what you get DONE!"

A journey of a thousand miles begins with (and is made up of) single steps no matter how big or small. If the steps and movement are consistent then they WILL get you there, a principle often referred to as "the Compound Effect".

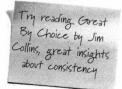

Try reading Great By Choice by Jim Collins, great insights about consistency

In my experience, awareness is the key. Once you have awareness of something, you have choice over it. You get to exercise your free will. There is no judgement from me on what you decide to do based upon what you THINK you can do. The choice is still yours but choice without act is just dreaming, work is required.

An idea that is developed and put into action is more important than an idea that exists only as an idea. - Buddah

SO, WHAT MAKES A GOOD BUSINESS IDEA WORTH BACKING?

1. It has to solve a real and pressing problem

2. The idea must provide value to a group of people who will pay for it (missed by many!)

3. There should be opportunities to leverage the product or service created to make it Scalable

4. Fast to test and prove on a small scale

5. One you can explain in a few short sentences so people " get it"

Let's face it, as a rule people don't like pain. For some, pain can be taking longer to do something that they don't like, discomfort (physical, emotional, social) or losing something that is of value to them. Studies show that as much as 80% of the population is Away From Motivated, good to know if you plan on launching a product.

Remember this by thinking — where there's, there's Profit!

People also like to feel good, about themselves, their lives, their future etc. This is often referred to as Towards Motivated. If you have an idea and a way to help people reduce or remove a pain and or gain more pleasure then you're definitely on the right track.

A Key point to remember here is that it's far more profitable if the idea solves a problem for a large group that is growing and has the means (resources, money, time, etc.) to pay more for the product or service than it costs to produce or provide it.

OK lets get into the "How to" part of the Chapter...

MONEY & MARGINS

PRACTICE STRATEGIES FOR IMPLEMENTING YOUR GREAT BUSINESS IDEAS

1. Write them down - words, pictures whatever suits your style to remember it. If you plan to share it or you will need help in developing it, then it is essential to put it into a format that others can understand and 'get' the concept. Speed of sharing also helps your idea get momentum and can help with testing it on a small scale as well.

2. Get an understanding of what level of protection for the intellectual property (IP) and design is appropriate. It's prudent to assess the risks and costs of protection before proceeding. Let's face it, if it really is a million pound/dollar idea, then it's worth spending the time and money to protect it. If it's an idea that will revolutionise the way something is done in your organisation, department or team, then it's worth making sure that you clearly establish that you've done your homework. This puts you in a stronger position and further establishes your value to the organisation. That said, "money loves speed" and there are times when you may not choose to wait for all of the i's and t's to be dotted and crossed. Just be sure that you're aware of and are prepared for the risks that come with moving that quickly – especially if you are in an environment where there are others that are better resourced, connected and positioned to 'steal your thunder'.

3. Talk it through - say it out loud. Sometimes just saying it out loud to yourself can change your perspective. Various levels of talking it through can be employed. You can discuss it in

   An Inner Circle of trusted people with insight from various angles such as that of a potential customer, business operations or marketing perspectives.

   Your mastermind group, business coach, mentor(s) are a great place to start. If you have ideas that you think are worth tens of thousands of pounds, then the investment of getting a coach is exactly that... an investment. Additionally, friends and family can also provide valuable feedback

   An Outer Circle of people that are early adopters to broaden the test group/ Again, you should consider the various perspectives.

Social media communities (closed or private) are a great place to test out concepts. Also if you are part of a business networking and professional development group such as The Business Wealth Club where there is a high level of trust, integrity and confidentiality, this too is a great place to test out your ideas and get balanced feedback.

4. Focus on the CONCEPT. This goes back to Plato, the philosopher, in discussing 'the ideal' and 'the form'. By doing this you are forming a strong tie with the outcome that you want to achieve, leaving room for the receptacle or 'details' to change as you develop the idea. Too often, people get so caught up and emotionally tied to the end product (details), that when the end product is sent to other people for the purpose of critique, the person who formed the idea becomes unwilling to change the end product because of emotional reasons. This is despite the fact that the form and concept would be better achieved if the suggestions were taken on board though they may or may not compromise the outcome, essence or concept that was the source of the design/process or product.

As best selling Author of *Rich Dad Poor Dad* and creator of the Cash Flow Quadrant Robert Kiasakie teaches – Business and Investing is a Team Sport, so understating "who" you need around you to help get your idea implemented is critical to your success.

Your 'dream team' may already be closer than you think. To make sure that your Team is balanced, I recommend using a tool like the Talent Dynamics model. If you haven't heard of Talent Dynamics before, find out more at:

www.marcelluslindsay.com/profiletest

If you already know the model – your Team needs three profiles over to the left and three profiles over to the right. That will make sense when you've visited this website ù

It's important to have close and trusted 'counsel' that will see things from different perspectives for you to weigh up. They can also take the idea through 'destruction testing' to allow you to

MONEY & MARGINS

find holes or flaws that are best discovered, discussed and addressed before the stakes are too high (i.e. taken to market, decision makers or investors)

You may also assemble an informal or unofficial review board of inner circle people BUT not inform them that they are doing anything in an official capacity. I have found in the past that the moment you ask someone to do it in a formal way, his or her creativity and perspective changes from the original way you wanted them to contribute. Doing it informally and unofficially allows them to relax, stay in flow and contribute in a far more productive and beneficial way.

There are a few people and resources to consider as part of your inner circle as you develop your ideas. You also have the added formal confidentiality protection that may not exist elsewhere

1. Business Coach – who is trained to ask you questions and guide you to ask yourself the important questions.

2. Business Mentor – somebody who has been there before you and who understands the risks and pit falls and is experienced enough to help you avoid them!

As you develop your idea it's a good idea to build a Power Team around you, that starts with your Business Coach or Mentor but which also includes:

1. Solicitor - who has an understanding of or specialises in IP protection, you don't want anybody stealing your good ideas now do you?

2. Project Manager - to help structure the way it can be methodically implemented adding rigor, assurance, risk management, measures of success and lessons (continuous improvement) knowledge application to each stage

3. Finance and investment – An Accountant with Strong Tax and Business Structure skills...

4. Marketing – someone with proven skills and an understanding of how and where to share the message, although this really should be YOUR area to own as you know the product or service better than anybody and what will motivate people to buy

HOW TO KEEP THE GOOD IDEAS COMING

1. Give yourself the gift of space and time. Schedule regular holidays or time away from the normal routine. Fun or Free days on a Friday can work well as we teach our Business Wealth Club Members to do.

2. Buy a special journal to write your ideas down and review them on a regular basis. There's even a pen (Livescribe) that can capture your handwritten notes and audio so that you can store and search the ideas on your computer later.

   This is such a cool tool and saves you so much time!

3. Use technology to help you catalogue your ideas. There are a number of applications including Evernote (for PC, MAC, iPhone, Android and web) or Microsoft One Note that can capture your ideas as audio, typed or images.

4. Join a business networking and professional development club. (Well I would say that wouldn't I) This is a great way to see what challenges and problems exist in other businesses. Maybe you can provide a solution that could be a new stream of income!

5. Work with your Business Coach or Business Mentor to identify problems that you'll face, solutions to the problems and to assess the value of the solutions to others.

6. Contact me for a no obligation, *30 minute session to find out more* Marcellus.Lindsay@thebusinesswealthclub.com I'll also be able to provide you with links and resources to get some of the tools mentioned in this chapter at a discount.

What are some of your ideas that, if you implemented them, could generate additional income for you, your family and your business? If you haven't written them down, do it now. If you have... what are you waiting for?

Remember that even the most talented person can't get by on talent alone. Whether they are an artist, athlete or entrepreneur, the most successful OUTSTANDING individuals get a coach, a team and surround themselves with like-minded people. That's the winning strategy that can work for you too.

Whatever your idea remember that Implementation = Income and that nothing was every achieved without help and hard work.

THINKING LONG TERM ABOUT
YOUR FINANCIAL FUTURE HAS
NEVER BEEN MORE IMPORTANT,
NOT SECURING THIS COULD
LEAVE YOU WITH SERIOUS
PROBLEMS. LET US SHOW YOU
HOW TO GET YOUR MONEY
WORKING HARDER FOR YOU...

LEVER
INVES

AGED
TMENT

NICK CARLILE

Nick Carlile is one of the three founders of *Platinum Partners*, a group of companies that offer wealth education, creation and protection with a keen focus on property.

A qualified Quantity Surveyor, Nick has worked in the property construction and investment industry since the age of 16. From building his own home in Yorkshire to managing large-scale international development projects worth tens of millions, Nick has a wealth of experience in the field.

In July 2007 he and his business partner, Steve Bolton, founded Platinum Property Partners, the world's first property investment franchise. This company went on to become one of the fastest growing franchises in UK history and continues to help its partners to invest into UK property in the most profitable way possible.

One of the other Platinum Partners companies, Platinum Portfolio Builder builds property portfolios for people who want to invest in property but who don't have the time, skill or inclination to do it themselves.

Nick alongside his fellow founding Partners are active Patrons of Peace one Day www.peaceoneday.org and through the Platinum Partners Foundation, support orphanages in Uganda & India and many other community projects in the UK.

MAXIMISING
YOUR RETURNS FROM
PROPERTY

I first met Nick and Steve, the founders of *Platinum Property Partners*, as they were just starting out on the exciting process of franchising their business - and I can say hand on heart that they are one of the most professional organisations I have ever coached. Now that their Franchise is booming - I am flattered to have been asked to speak and train at their high energy Franchisee meetings on a number of occasions.

In this so called depressed housing market - PPB, Nick's new business, are going from strength to strength. Proof if you ever needed it that a great Business will always succeed.

I really would encourage you to visit their web site www.platinumportfoliobuilder.co.uk and if you simply mention me... you can get hold of their book absolutely free!

— *Paul Avins*

> Property is an extremely complex business but in spite of this I meet people all of the time that watch Sarah Beeny on Thursday night and on Friday morning call themselves property developers or investors.

It's like me watching ER and then deciding to have a little go at open heart surgery. The results can be just as catastrophic (albeit financially) for those wannabe investors as they would be for me as a surgeon.

I have been investing in property since 1993 and have learned (and continue to learn) my trade from the many experiences, training, and mentors along the way. Due to the complexity of the subject and the limit on the number of words for this chapter I'm going to focus on a key fundamental of maximising returns from property. (I have also written my own book on this subject with more words in it!)

BUYING AT THE RIGHT PRICE

It sounds an obvious point to make - it's certainly something you hear trotted out whenever people talk about making money from property: "It's all in the buying". And that's true, particularly if you're looking to gain instant equity and recycle your capital as quickly as possible. By 'the right price', I mean the price that works for your investment strategy, and that 'right price' can change, depending on what you're buying.

If your strategy is about maximising equity, then the 'right' price is going to be 20% or more below what the property has been valued at.

If your strategy is cashflow then you may be prepared to pay full asking price, if the property gives you the great returns that you are looking for.

If your strategy is to buy an existing property or properties because you can see massive development potential and are confident the ultimate profit will be significant, then the 'right' price to guarantee you secure your purchase may be over the asking price.

> Know your strategy when buying each and every property. *Buy and Hope* is not a strategy!

One of my mentors said to me 'Nick, every property that you own has to have a clear reason for being in your portfolio' and this has stuck with me ever since. The reasons can be different for each property but they have to be clear.

> Every property that you own has to have a clear reason for being in your portfolio

But whatever your strategy, buying at the right price absolutely depends on your being able to identify the true value of the property, and in order to be able to do that, you need to know your own market inside out, to make sure you don't fall headlong into a big mistake.

When I hear people talk about The UK Property Market it's kind of like people asking what the weather in the UK is like. Each country, county, city, town, village, suburb or even street can and often is different. Within the UK there are literally thousands of property markets and it's the detailed knowledge and experience of those individual markets that will stop you making expensive mistakes.

LEVERAGED INVESTMENTS

BMV - BELOW MARKET VALUE

This is a term that's used in property networking events, seminars and courses up and down the UK and we have a bit of an issue with it, because it's a subjective term and completely open to interpretation. Does 'market value' mean the asking price, the estate agent's valuation, the price that's been offered by someone else, or a surveyor's valuation? Too many people over the past decade have been lured into buying property at supposedly a massive discount, only to discover that it was never actually worth what they'd been told its true value was and the huge chunk of equity they believed they would have never materialises.

SURVEYED VALUE AND BSVS

The closest you can get to a 'true' valuation is to have an independent RICS surveyor give you an open market valuation at the particular time you're looking to purchase. (To be accurate, a property is worth what someone will pay for it, but a RICS valuation is the next best thing!)

And because of precisely this issue, we actually don't call the strategy of buying property at a discount BMV; we refer to BSV – Below Surveyed Value – because that's the only valuation that matters. While 'Market Value' is subjective and open to interpretation and manipulation, 'Surveyed Value' is a fact.

DUE DILIGENCE

Often, people are so dazzled by the figures – the good seems so good – that they don't probe deeply enough into the worst case scenario. I'll say it again – you have to make sure you're buying at the right price for your strategy, and unless you check out the investment thoroughly, you could end up paying over the odds if it doesn't deliver what you thought it would. I call it 'stress-testing' the numbers. With a buy to let property, some of the key things you should be asking yourself are:

What happens if the discount isn't what I thought it was?

What happens if I don't get 100% occupancy?

Have I factored in the fact it may take several months to get the property ready to rent?

What happens if interest rates climb?

What happens if the market doesn't double in value every 7-10 years?

What happens if house prices fall in the next 12 months?

What happens if rents fall?

What happens if I can't sell a property once it's completed?

What happens if I find myself competing with all the other investors who also bought into the same development?

What happens if...? What happens if...? What happens if...?

Work your figures – we have very sophisticated spreadsheets we use to analyse numerous different scenarios – so that we can be absolutely confident the offer we're making on a property means it's going to work financially in the way we want and we've built in a big enough cushion to allow for the variables. Just get in touch and we'll be happy to share these with you.

And always be aware of alternative strategies so you have a 'Plan B' in case 'Plan A' doesn't work out. i.e. if your strategy is to buy at a discount and then sell, what happens if the market turns, what happens if the discount isn't viable – are you able to rent it, can you do a lease option, can you find a tenant buyer...?

PORTFOLIO BUILDING SERVICES – WHAT'S THE RIGHT PRICE?

If you are busy focusing on another business or your employment you may want to consider asking for experts to help you invest into property. Do your own diligence and ask around.

Building a portfolio isn't something you can do overnight, and if you want to really maximise the profitability of the properties you own or control, that takes a lot of time. Learning how to source, negotiate, acquire, refurbish, tenant and manage those properties to get the best return on your investment takes years of practice and experience.

That's where investment companies come in, essentially offering you a short cut to success.

> **Stand on the shoulders of giants, as the saying goes - but it's imperative you understand that while you can leapfrog the experience/expertise element, you can't shortcut the time it takes to do diligence.**

I'm going to stick this up on my wall!

One of the keys to a successful long-term partnership is the service provider having a vested interest in ensuring the investments are sound, there's a robust strategy behind the property business and the portfolio is consistently profitable.

Be really, really wary of any company that makes all their profit at the front end. The up-front fee we charge for our Platinum Portfolio Builder covers our costs with the majority of our profit coming at the back end, with a 75%/25% equity split between the investor and us. That way, we're incentivised to buy right: something with both in-built equity and the strong likelihood of good capital growth.

The area we invest in is where I have lived and worked virtually all of my life, and I know the market better than most. During 2010 we purchased over £8.1 million worth of property for a total cost of just over £6 million. That's an instant equity of £2.1 million and a discount of around 26% and these properties were delivered to our clients under our Platinum Portfolio Builder brand. We retain a vested interest in every property that we buy and that way our clients know that if it's the wrong investment for them, it's the wrong investment for us. That win-win relationship is something we truly believe in.

Buying at the right price is just a tiny part of successful property investing but it's a good place to start.

NEXT STEPS

Know your strategy and ensure that the reason why you are buying the property matches this.

'Stress test' your figures and work out what the 'right' price is to buy at for your strategy to effectively deliver the returns you want.

Double and triple check any 'BMV' leads you're offered and make sure the discounts are verified by an independent RICS qualified surveyor.

Be prepared to pay a fair price for a good opportunity: cost verses value.

Always visit the investment location, whether it's Barnsley or Barbados. There is nothing quite like seeing it for yourself.

If it sounds too good to be true, then it usually is!

If you would like to find out more about Nick and Platinum Portfolio Builder simply call 01226 732606 or visit the website at

www.platinumportfoliobuilder.co.uk

Make sure you mention Paul Avins and you will be sent a free copy of Nick's bestselling book which has great content, hints and tips and mistakes to avoid when considering property investment

LEVERAGED INVESTMENTS

MARCUS
DE MARIA

Marcus is a well respected stock market and wealth educator, financially independent, and fulfilling his purpose in life which is to teach others how to do the same. But it wasn't always like this. Not too many years ago Marcus was living on his brother's floor and over £100,000 in debt. He realised that the thinking that got him into this situation was not going to be the same to get him out of the situation.

He gave up the security of a well-paid though unfulfilling job to train with coaching legend Anthony Robbins in 1999. In 2003 he started his own training business, Investment Mastery, to train total beginners how to make consistent profits investing and training in the stock market www.investment-mastery.com. In 2005 he launched the Wealth Workout, his flagship wealth creation seminar, bringing general wealth training to families around UK and started teaching the materials in schools www.wealth-workout.com.

Marcus has recently teamed up with T Harv Eker to teach his Millionaire Mind Intensives in UK, Europe and Asia and other more advanced wealth creation seminars.

Training is very different to public speaking and Marcus is fast becoming one of UK's most experienced and exciting trainers.

STOCK MARKET INVESTING
FOR BUSINESS OWNERS

Marcus and I have been friends ever since we met at an event in London called Millionaire Mind where I was MC for the weekend and he was one of the speakers. Since that time we've spoken at each others events, me at his Wealth Workout weekend and him at the Business Wealth Club Open Days. We've promoted each others books and helped countless people increase their Net Worth.

He's now become a Global Trainer as part of T Harv Ekers team running Millionaire Mind Intensive weekends and I am delighted at his success. His skill is to take the daunting work of Stocks & Shares Investing and teach it in a format everybody can learn.... if they choose to, and the returns can be very impressive! I hope you'll add him to your list of Wealth Advisors as I have done!

— *Paul Avins*

> The stock market is the most misunderstood of all wealth vehicles. The city boys don't want us to know just how simple it is to make money trading and investing. And no wonder - they only benefit if you give them your money to trade and invest.

When I first heard about the stock market in a public seminar in London back in 1999, I learned that you can make money when markets go up AND down. I still don't know any other wealth creation vehicle that allows you to make money when markets go down! With this in mind, the message is simple - no matter how little time you as a business owner think you have or don't have, investing and growing your money must be a part of your personal wealth creation strategy. You can thank me later.

What is the difference between trading and investing? Trading takes advantage of short term price movements, up and down, where you look to *time the market* in both market directions. You might own the stock for a few days or weeks only. You are not focused on the fundamental health of a company in the way an investor is. Investing means you want to be a shareholder of the company because you believe in its growth potential, its management etc. Investors aren't interested in short term trading, they know that most of the money is made through the longer term 'time IN the market'.

Personally, I do both because I want to be able to take advantage of both market directions, not just 'up'. Imagine my surprise when in 2003 I discovered that there was a 3rd market direction, sideways. So there are 3 market movements not 2: up, down and sideways. Most fund managers only invest in one market direction, up. That way they have only 1 in 3 chance of making money. Can you see now why many of them have a problem growing your money? Just by learning how to make money going down (called selling short) you have increased your chances to 2 in 3. And if you learn all 3 ... that's even better!

There are so many strategies out there. Best to keep it simple. Learn one or two simple strategies that fit into your busy lifestyle and make you money alongside your business.

Keep it simple!

BUSINESS OWNERS: IGNORE YOUR PERSONAL FINANCES AT YOUR PERIL

I meet so many business people who are focused solely on growing their businesses. Unfortunately they don't focus on their own net worth and so if anything happens to the business – and I've met a few – they are left with nothing.

So my message is simple. Do both. Make some effort on a Friday afternoon for half an hour in the stock market to grow your personal assets via trading, investing or both. Don't do it and you might live to regret it, often when it is too late to do anything about it.

And I don't mean giving your money away to someone else to invest either. No one cares about your money as much as you do. Also, once you learn this skill, you have it forever and can teach your friends and family so they can start younger and take advantage of the power of compounding from a much earlier age.

NOT A CASE OF *IF*, BUT A CASE OF *WHICH STRATEGY*

I am here to tell you in no uncertain terms that you must look into the stock market as an additional stream of financial wealth. It is not a case of IF, it is rather a case of WHICH strategy suits your lifestyle. Here's why. You don't deal with staff or customers; you can do it anytime anywhere as long as you have internet access; It is totally recession proof, in fact you can make money faster when markets go down; You are in total control and able to sell your stocks within 4-5 seconds at the price you want – these are liquid markets and there are always buyers and sellers. Try selling your business in 4-5 months at the price you want let alone 4-5 seconds. Not an easy task.

LEVERAGED INVESTMENTS

WHERE ELSE CAN YOU COMPOUND YOUR MONEY EVERY MONTH?

You will have heard about the magic that is compound growth. Alongside your business, have an additional pot which is growing through compounding. You never take out any profits – unless you have to – but you can put more in to really compound your money. Personally I would like to see you do this as a minimum: Start off with as close to £5,000 or more, save £10 a day, get 13% return or more a year with our help and have an additional £2,000,000 alongside your business to retire on. That way you can live off the interest and still keep the £2,000,000. Fantastic stuff.

Initial amount to invest:	£5,000
% Return a Year	1.13%
How much can you save a day	£10 (£3,650/year)

Age 30	40	50	60	70
£5,650	£86,411	£360,561	£1,291,182	£4,450,236
£10,035	£101,295	£411,084	£1,462,686	£5,032,417
£14,989	£118,113	£468,175	£1,656,485	£5,690,281
£20,588	£137,118	£532,688	£1,875,478	£6,433,668
£26,914	£158,593	£605,588	£2,122,940	£7,273,695
£34,063	£182,860	£687,964	£2,402,572	£8,222,925
£42,141	£210,282	£781,049	£2,718,556	£9,295,555
£51,269	£241,269	£886,236	£3,075,619	£10,507,627
£61,584	£276,284	£1,005,096	£3,479,099	£11,877,269
£73,240	£315,851	£1,139,409	£3,935,032	£13,424,964

> The best time to start is now – compounding waits for no-one.

Start now or wake up one day and it is too late. Where to start? I prefer to go where the most money can be made, which is the biggest and most liquid markets, i.e. the US but you can invest in the UK also. I do both. Simply choose an online discount broker where you only need your laptop to invest.

> Consider wrapping up your money in an ISA or a SIPP so you don't pay any taxes – this will allow you to compound your money faster.

Great Wealth Tip!

CONCEPT: VALUE COST AVERAGE

Many people have heard of Pound Cost Averaging, where you buy the same amount of stock every month at the same time. The benefit of this is that unlike someone who puts all their money in at the same time once and might buy at a very expensive price, PCA means you are buying at different price points, which avoids you buying right at the top of any market.

If you add just one more step you can improve on this using a technique which I call Value Cost Averaging (VCA). Here you put the same amount of money in each month also but in the months where the stock falls, you put in a little extra. That way your average price is even lower and when the turnaround comes, you will be in a lower average price to benefit.

SOME VERY BASIC STRATEGIES

STRATEGY 1

Find out the value of a company and wait until it falls 40-50% below that value. That's what is so great about the market – it has wild mood swings, so you just wait patiently until it has one. Don't worry if you don't find anything for a while. Warren Buffett, the most famous and successful investor of all time might not make a trade for a whole year.

STRATEGY 2

Wait for a market correction, called a bear market. Based on past bear markets, around 2 years into the bear market, when the markets start to bottom out, start buying pieces of your favourite strategy using the value cost average concept outlined below.

STRATEGY 3

Look at companies that have constant revenue like American water companies. There are very few surprises here so their stock price tends to go up and down, up and down and the result is a sideways movement for years on end. You can buy and sell these companies as they bob up and down for 10% a time several times a year. And once you learn 'Selling short', you can make money when markets go down aswell, thus doubling your percentage returns.

NEXT STEPS

The key to successful investing is to learn a strategy to suit your lifestyle and profile.

Go to:

www.investment-mastery.com

for more information on how to get started, we run 1 day Introductory Courses, Webinars and Teleseminars.

GAVIN HOLMES

Gavin has become recognized as a worldwide expert in the Volume Spread Analysis methodology and market manipulation. In his self-published book series called, "Trading in the Shadow of the Smart Money" Gavin discusses why market manipulation can actually be a good thing for traders and investors who can read the chart correctly based on universal laws. Also available is "Trading in the Shadow of the Smart Money Volume 2: Sequential VSA Chart Patterns Explained".

Gavin has been featured as a headline speaker at numerous seminars and webinars around the world. He has provided educational courses for the CME Group in Chicago and has been featured at the New York and Las Vegas traders expo's Traders Challenge where Gavin traded his live account, showing the principles of VSA appearing live and taking trades. Gavin's mission to educate traders and Investors to become experts in the lost art of chart reading and to understand the importance of volume the hidden secret of the markets. His passion is based on the original teachings of Richard Wyckoff, Richard Ney, and Tom Williams who all had the same goal, to educate the uninformed public.

HOW TO LOOSE MONEY
AS A TRADER
& INVESTOR

Gavin and I have been friends for nearly 10 years now and he still "blames" me for dragging him to the Anthony Robbins event *Unleash the Power Within* which started him on his Wealth Acceleration journey! He and I have worked together on a number of projects over the years and he was even an Investor in one of my Businesses which was great fun. In the last 5 years I have watched in wonder as he has taken the US by storm as a Stock Trading "Guru" and expert in understanding how the smart money moves the markets.

His enthusiasm for life, learning and helping people take control of their Financial Future is on a par with my passion for business, so when we get together, it's hard for anybody else to get a word in!

I have also had the opportunity to speak at one of his high ticket events in San Francisco and to have coached some of his team on internet marketing for their software, which is excellent by the way.

I am so glad that in between publishing his first and second books he found some time to share his Market Insights with you here. I've read his book and, trust me, this info is POWerful if a little controversial at times. All I care about is that it works for him and his clients and will work for you as well.

Grab a Coffee and hold on this is going to be a wild ride...

— *Paul Avins*

> Over the last 4 years I've trained thousands of Traders and Investors using our Value Spread Analysis System. It tracks the movements of the Smart Money (money from hedge Funds & the Mega Rich), which is what leads to Market Manipulation.

One of my most successful seminars was entitled *10 Ways Volume Spread Analysis Will Turn Losing Traders into Winning Traders* - how "Smart Money enabled trading can alert you to what is really happening in the market".

In this webinar I first listed the top 10 reasons, in my opinion, that the average retail trader and investor loses money when trading or investing. Here are the reasons, in no particular order of importance:

1. LOSING TRADERS/INVESTORS DO NOT HAVE A TRADING PLAN!

In my experience it is vital to have a plan when you trade or invest, just like in business or life. Without it, you have no measure of what you are doing or what's generating you good results or costing you cash.

Traders who loose money do different things on different days, and are totally inconsistent, so they never get to replicate their winning strategies and by the way... Luck is not a strategy to Trade on!

2. LOSING TRADERS/INVESTORS LACK BELIEF IN THEIR CHOSEN STRATEGY

Belief is key to your financial returns. Computers do not think, they compute the inputted information and are not driven by emotions. Your brain is a very powerful tool and when used correctly, will produce outstanding results.

3. LOSING TRADERS/INVESTORS THINK AND ACT LIKE GAMBLERS

A card counter that goes to Vegas puts the odds in his (or her) favour, which is why card counters are banned if discovered! As a trader or investor, you can put the odds in your favour if you study for a few hours each week to grow you skills. I've studied hard for over 4 years, been mentored by one of the worlds leading experts in Volume Spread Analysis and my returns have been BIG!

The more you Learn – the more you Earn.

4. LOSING TRADERS/INVESTORS ARE ALWAYS SEARCHING FOR THE HOLY GRAIL OF TRADING

The so called Silver Bullet that will help them make Easy Money - it doesn't exist.

How many trading software packages have you got that consistently make you money? How many times have slick sales and marketing of a product prompted you to buy based on their claims of percentage accuracy? How many times have you been taken for a MUG (Mathematically Uneducated Gambler!) when you thought you had found the "Holy Grail"? How many times have you asked yourself "Am I getting mugged by 'Smart Money' that understands my underlying reasons to take a trade?" (The reason usually being greed for more money, or fear of further loss when losing money.) Hey, welcome to the world of being a HUMAN BEING; it's natural, so learn to master your emotions!

5. LOSING TRADERS/INVESTORS OFTEN USE TOO MANY SYSTEMS AND TOO MANY INDICATORS

Have you ever suffered from 'analysis paralysis'? Are you looking at too many indicators and too many charts so that your brain becomes confused and clarity disappears? Keeping trading and investing as simple as possible using the tried and tested methods such as VSA and the Wyckoff method (any jargon and industry specific terms and products that I reference in this chapter are explained in my book - see the offer at the end of this chapter) will help you read the market as it unfolds. "The chart never lies, if you know how to read it correctly."

6. LOSING TRADERS/INVESTORS ARE OFTEN UNDER CAPITALIZED, TAKING LARGE TRADES WITH POOR RISK/REWARD RATIOS, AND NO MONEY MANAGEMENT SKILLS

Winning traders are traders with discipline, belief, lack of fear, and knowledge of how the markets work. They know they can never be 100% right, and they get out of losing positions quickly and see it as a small business loss, not a financial disaster. How do you treat losses?

7. LOSING TRADERS/INVESTORS DO NOT UNDERSTAND HOW MARKETS WORK, BELIEVING THAT PRICE MOVES MARKETS, IT DOESN'T

The forces of supply and demand and the trading of 'Smart Money' cause prices to move. Winning Traders have studied how the markets truly operate and know how to win the game they are in.

8. LOSING TRADERS/INVESTORS FALL FOR SLICK SALES AND MARKETING OF TRADING SYSTEMS THAT CLAIM TO HAVE A HIGH PERCENTAGE OF ACCURACY, CONFUSE LOSING TRADERS

They end up trying many systems that almost always result is losses. Have you ever heard the sales guy tell you, "Our system is 80% accurate - it's so easy to trade with our system a seven year old can do it!! Just follow the three green lights and buy, three red lights and sell"? How many times HAVE YOU been burned?

9. LOSING TRADERS/INVESTORS ALWAYS FOLLOW THE HERD, AND GET LOCKED IN TO BAD TRADES!

How can you prevent yourself being a HERD member and being led to the slaughter by 'Smart Money'? If you could truly understand HOW to read a price chart correctly how quickly could you become profitable?

Zig when others Zag

In my experiences It's all about DISCIPLINE.
Fortunately, you don't have to be a genius to be a successful trader/investor. As Berkshire Hathaway chief and investor extraordinaire, Warren Buffett said in a 1999 interview with Business Week:

> "Success in investing doesn't correlate with IQ once you're above the level of 25. Once you have ordinary intelligence, what you need is the temperament to control the urges that get other people into trouble in investing."

It's true that not everyone is gifted with Buffett's calm, cool demeanour. Challenging yourself to avoid your own worst instincts will help you reach your financial goals.

Winning Traders And Investors Have The Following Characteristics:

- Self Belief

- Visualisation of Success – seeing the winners/cutting losers

- Contrarian – think as an individual

LEVERAGED INVESTMENTS

261

- Expert chart reading skills

- Highly disciplined

- Spiritual – Have a Purpose bigger than just getting more Cash

- Open minded and willing to help others

- Expect to receive and do so graciously

- Excellent risk management strategies

- Always able to stay in the game!! NEVER risk more than they can afford to loose

- Take consistent and small profits – NOT GREEDY.

- Are always happy and content Playing the Game

It is easy to get into the market, you don't need magic words like "open sesame", just a computer, an internet connection, a brokerage account, and some charting tools, but knowing when to get OUT is the key.

Greed and excitement will always cost you money. You must become the master of your emotions and each time you trade and invest, follow your plan with military precision, knowing exactly what you will do if anything goes wrong and the trade is not working.

POINTS TO CONSIDER...

Volume Spread Analysis (VSA™) seeks to establish the cause of price movements. The 'cause', quite simply, is the imbalance between supply and demand (or Strength and Weakness) in a liquid market. However, what most people don't know is the markets don't move by accident. They are deliberately manipulated to wrong-foot the unsuspecting 'herd', or uninformed traders and the VSA methodology and TradeGuider Systems' software helps you understand how to trade in harmony with these market movements.

Whether we admit it or not, human beings are conditioned to act as a herd and the media unwittingly play a key role in helping investors and traders form an opinion about traded instruments such as stocks, commodities, futures, or even Forex. Like a twisted version of mass hysteria, when media-induced opinions about traded instruments are 'suggested', the majority of the uninformed herd believe these opinions as fact and it will end up costing them dearly.

So don't forget: Beware of the news! It is not necessarily that the media are lying; they are simply reporting what they are told.

> As Mark Twain once said, "If you do not read the newspaper, you are uninformed, and if you do read the newspaper, you are misinformed."

Volume is the key to the truth- ignore it at your peril. The truth is in the chart if you know how to read it and that's what I will teach you.

NEXT STEPS

To Download 4 Free Chapters from Gavin's Book – Trading in the shadow of the Smart Money go to:

www.tradingintheshadow.com

To Learn more about TradeGuider Software go to:

www.tradeguider.com

for a Free Trial.

LEVERAGED INVESTMENTS

SIMON ZUTSHI

Simon Zutshi, who is a financially independent property millionaire, was able to retire from conventional employment at the age of 32 thanks to the passive income generated from his property portfolio. He has been investing in property since 1995 and in 2003 he set up the Property Investors Network to provide a supportive environment to help people become successful property investors.

He now spends most of his time educating people on how they can become financially independent through property investing.

One of Simons passions is professional speaking. His main topic is property investing, but he also speaks on wealth creation, passive income, business growth and internet marketing. Simon is a member of the Professional Speakers Association PSA and National Speakers Association NSA.

FINANCIAL FREEDOM THROUGH
PROPERTY INVESTING

My connection to Simon goes back longer than I care to remember! We first met up as members of the Professional Speakers Association in the UK and discovered we had a mutual friend. Simon was coaching on property at the time and having seen him speak I asked him to be one of our first ever speakers at our now famous (well in Oxfordshire anyway) Business Wealth Club Open Days.

He's helped a number of my key clients build property portfolio's over the years and Sue and Angela also took his weekend workshop several years ago. We have shared stages and promoted each other's events and I have even done some Strategic Consulting for his PIN Network in the past.

I consider him a good friend, especially as we both turned 40 in the same year, and apparently life is only just beginning now for us both - watch out world!

— *Paul Avins*

All successful business people recognise that it is wise to reinvest some of the surplus profits from their business to get their cash working for them. There are many different types of investment vehicles and assets available however there is one asset class that the rich and successful people chose over any other and that is property investing.

> **You do not need to be rich to reap the benefits of property investing. Indeed the really successful investors understand that you can make money from property using other people's money.**

A key point to learn!

One of the attractions of property investing is that the long term trend for property prices is up. This is due to simple supply and demand, the fact that we have a shortage of accommodation in the UK and an increasing demand due to a growing population. However property prices are cyclical. Just like every other market, prices go down as well as up!

From the early 2000's the UK property market experienced a boom until prices reached a peak in October 2007. At this point, the two main groups of buyers who stimulate the market (first time buyers and buy to let investors) stopped buying because the property prices were just too high.

As a result, property prices fell by an average of 20% by the end of 2009. The UK media was full of doom and gloom about the property market and indeed it was not a good time to be selling a property. But property investors don't sell property, they buy. So now is actually a great time to invest as long as you know what you are doing and always do your research to make sure you buy the right property.

If you are buying property over the next few years there are a few golden rules you need to obey:

1. Always buy below market value from a motivated seller, somebody in pain and in a hurry to sell

2. Buy in an area with strong rental demand so that you can easily and quickly rent it out

3. Only buy property that will give you a positive cash flow each month
    DO NOT BREAK THIS ONE!

4. Remember you are investing for the long term of at least five years

5. Have a cash buffer to cover any unexpected expenses or Void rent periods

The fundamental principle is that you buy a property, and then let it out to some tenants who pay you rent to live there. The idea being that the tenants cover all of your costs of ownership and also give you some positive cash flow. In addition to this cash flow, you get the benefit of significant capital growth as the property increases in value over time.

The hardest part is finding the right property in the first place which does require some time and effort (although you can get other people to help you with this). But once you have found the property most of the work is over. You can delegate the day to day management to a third party such as a letting agent. In this way property investing is an example of working once and then getting paid forever.

LEVERAGED INVESTMENTS

Currently, for a typical buy to let investment, you need a 25% deposit (although this does not have to be your own money) and you can obtain a 75% mortgage. This mortgage is not dependant on your income but rather on the amount of rental income generated from the property. However your personal credit score will be important as lenders have tightened their lending criteria since the Credit Crunch, so work to keep it in tip top shape.

> The key to successful buy to let investing is to purchase a property in a location where there is strong rental demand and the rent "Stacks up". This means that the rent is enough to cover all of the costs and still leave a profit for you at the end of each month.

Each year you will have to pay income tax on your rental profit, so be sure to get good accounting advice!

With all these costs and the hassle of finding and managing a property, you may be thinking "why do people do it for just a small profit each month?" The answer is they don't! Most people invest for the long term capital growth. Historically over the last 60 years property has double in value on average every 7 to 9 years. It may take a while to recover from the last crash so let's say it takes 10 to 12 years for prices to double again from now.

> If you have a £100k property now it could be worth £200k in just 10 years time. If you had put a 25% deposit into the property your investment would have been £25k and the capital gain would be £100k.

That is a fantastic 400% return on investment. You would not get that kind of return in a bank, in the stock market or in fact any other form of investment which is why property investing is one of the best investments you can possibly make.

NEXT STEPS

To find out more about how you could profit from investing in property a great first step would be to get a copy of my book 'Property Magic' which is an Amazon No 1 best seller.

In the book I describe how you can build a property portfolio using other people's time money and experience.

Here's the offer: to get a complimentary copy of the book all you need to do is to visit this website and pay for the post and packaging:

www.propertymagicbook.com/free

LEVERAGED INVESTMENTS

THE BUSINESS WEALTH CLUB

Learn why our unique **Business Growth Community** is attracting Business Owners to Join our Clubs at *record levels...*

Professional Networking & Joint Ventures

Blended Training & Coaching

Positive Local Support

To find out more go to **www.TheBusinessWealthClub.com**

BECOME A MENTOR OF YOUR OWN BUSINESS WEALTH CLUB

I chose to become a BWC mentor for four reasons:

1. To help local businesses grow. There is very little specific and practical support to grow a business for small business owners and entrepreneurs.

2. I like working with businesses where you can discuss things on a Monday and by Friday they are implemented. Small business owners have the power to see it's done quickly.

You Get Paid on what you get....DONE!

3. To learn from like minded mentors and coaches. I have always been interested in personal development and found the team at BWC have great ideas and content.

4. To grow my businesses. To practise what I preach. Running a club has given me the opportunity to share and give back. I've gained some interesting insights from the members, boosted my network of contacts as well as positioned myself better in the marketplace

— *Alan French,*
Mentor at St. Albans Business Wealth Club

NOTES

SUNMAKERS

Publish your expertise

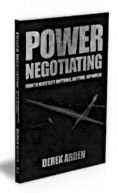

www.sunmakers.co.uk

Lightning Source UK Ltd.
Milton Keynes UK
UKOW041620110113

204765UK00001BB/6/P